PERSPECTIVES ON WRITING
Series Editor, Susan H. McLeod

PERSPECTIVES ON WRITING
Series Editor, Susan H. McLeod

The Perspectives on Writing series addresses writing studies in a broad sense. Consistent with the wide ranging approaches characteristic of teaching and scholarship in writing across the curriculum, the series presents works that take divergent perspectives on working as a writer, teaching writing, administering writing programs, and studying writing in its various forms.

The WAC Clearinghouse and Parlor Press are collaborating so that these books will be widely available through free digital distribution and low-cost print editions. The publishers and the Series editor are teachers and researchers of writing, committed to the principle that knowledge should freely circulate. We see the opportunities that new technologies have for further democratizing knowledge. And we see that to share the power of writing is to share the means for all to articulate their needs, interest, and learning into the great experiment of literacy.

Recent Books in the Series

Tara Roeder and Roseanne Gatto (Eds.), *Critical Expressivism: Theory and Practice in the Composition Classroom* (2014)

Terry Myers Zawacki and Michelle Cox (Eds), *WAC and Second-Language Writers: Research Towards Linguistically and Culturally Inclusive Programs and Practices*, (2014)

Charles Bazerman, *A Rhetoric of Literate Action: Literate Action Volume 1* (2013)

Charles Bazerman, *A Theory of Literate Action: Literate Action Volume 2* (2013)

Katherine V. Wills and Rich Rice (Eds.), *ePortfolio Performance Support Systems: Constructing, Presenting, and Assessing Portfolios* (2013)

Mike Duncan and Star Medzerian Vanguri (Eds.), *The Centrality of Style* (2013)

Chris Thaiss, Gerd Bräuer, Paula Carlino, Lisa Ganobcsik-Williams, and Aparna Sinha (Eds.), *Writing Programs Worldwide: Profiles of Academic Writing in Many Places* (2012)

Andy Kirkpatrick and Zhichang Xu, *Chinese Rhetoric and Writing: An Introduction for Language Teachers* (2012)

Doreen Starke-Meyerring, Anthony Paré, Natasha Artemeva, Miriam Horne, and Larissa Yousoubova (Eds.), *Writing in Knowledge Societies* (2011)

BEYOND DICHOTOMY: SYNERGIZING WRITING CENTER AND CLASSROOM PEDAGOGIES

Steven J. Corbett

The WAC Clearinghouse
wac.colostate.edu
Fort Collins, Colorado

Parlor Press
www.parlorpress.com
Anderson, South Carolina

The WAC Clearinghouse, Fort Collins, Colorado 80523-1052
Parlor Press, 3015 Brackenberry Drive, Anderson, South Carolina 29621

Printed in the United States of America

Library of Congress Cataloging-in-Publication Data Pending

Copyeditor: Don Donahue
Designer: Mike Palmquist
Series Editor: Susan H. McLeod

Cover Image: Roman Republic coin showing Janus, c. 225-212 BCE; Kunsthistorisches Museum, Vienna; Photo by Jona Lendering (livius.org)

This book is printed on acid-free paper.

The WAC Clearinghouse supports teachers of writing across the disciplines. Hosted by Colorado State University, it brings together scholarly journals and book series as well as resources for teachers who use writing in their courses. This book is available in digital format for free download at http://wac.colostate.edu.

Parlor Press, LLC is an independent publisher of scholarly and trade titles in print and multimedia formats. This book is available in print and digital formats from Parlor Press at http://www.parlorpress.com. For submission information or to find out about Parlor Press publications, write to Parlor Press, 3015 Brackenberry Drive, Anderson, South Carolina 29621, or email editor@parlorpress.com.

For Michelle, my favorite

CONTENTS

BEYOND DICHOTOMY: SYNERGIZING WRITING CENTER AND CLASSROOM PEDAGOGIES

ACKNOWLEDGMENTS

This book would not have been possible without the support and kindness of many people. I'd like to thank David Blakesley for entertaining the original proposal and encouraging me to submit it to the Perspectives on Writing Series. Huge thank you to Sue McLeod and Mike Palmquist for believing in this project from the start and for their patient and thoughtful guidance throughout the publication process. Thank you to the anonymous reviewers for their detailed and constructive feedback, which helped tremendously in reining in a wild-horse of an early draft. And special thanks to Paul Rogers, my west-coast brother in spirit. Many energizing conversations with Paul helped me to perform essential fine-tunings for clarity, precision, and purposefulness throughout the book.

Finally, thank you will never be enough Pat Marks, Teagan Decker, Anis Bawarshi, Juan Guerra, George Dillon, Gail Stygall, and Will Hochman for opening the gates and allowing me in.

INTRODUCTION

SHARING PEDAGOGICAL AUTHORITY: PRACTICE COMPLICATES THEORY WHEN SYNERGIZING CLASSROOM, SMALL-GROUP, AND ONE-TO-ONE WRITING INSTRUCTION

> In short, we are not here to serve, supplement, back up, complement, reinforce, or otherwise be defined by any external curriculum.
>
> – Stephen North

> Our field can no longer afford, if it ever could, to have forged a separate peace between classroom and nonclassroom teaching. There is no separate but equal.
>
> – Elizabeth H. Boquet and Neal Lerner

> The intersecting contexts of on-location tutoring not only serve ...
>
> – Holly Bruland

Increasingly, the literature on writing centers and peer tutoring programs reports on what we've learned about teaching one-to-one and peer-to-peer from historical, theoretical, and empirical points of view. We've re-defined and re-interpreted just how far back the "desire for intimacy" in writing instruction really goes (Lerner "Teacher-Student," *The Idea*). We've questioned what counts as credible and useful research methods and methodologies (Babcock and Thonus; Liggett, Jordan, and Price; Corbett "Using," "Negotiating") and meaningful assessment (Schendel and Macauley). We've explored what the implications of peer tutoring are, for not just tutees, but also for tutors themselves (Hughes, Gillespie, and Kail). And we've made connections to broader implications for the teaching and learning of writing (for example see Harris "Assignments," and Soliday *Everyday Genres* on assignment design and implementation; Greenfield and Rowan, Corbett, Lewis, and Clifford, and Denny on race and identity; Mann, and Corbett "Disability" on learning-disabled students; Lerner *The Idea* and Corbett, LaFrance, and Decker on the connections between writing center theory and practice and peer-to-peer learning in the writing classroom). Since the first publication of North's often-cited essay "The Idea of a Writing Center," quoted above, writing center practitioners and scholars have continued to ask a pivotal question: How closely can or should writing centers, writing classrooms—and the people involved in either or both—collaborate (North "Revisting"; Smith; Hemmeter; Healy; Raines; Soliday "Shifting Roles"; Decker; Sherwood; Boquet and Lerner)?

Yet with all our good intentions, unresolved tensions and dichotomies pervade all our actions as teachers or tutors of writing. At the heart of everything we do reside choices. Foremost among these choices includes just how directive (or interventionist or controlling) versus how nondirective (or noninterventionist or facilitative) we wish to be in the learning of any given student or group of students at any given time. The intricate balancing act between giving a student a fish and teaching him or her how to fish can be a very slippery art to grasp. But it is one we need to think about carefully, and often. It affects how we design and enact writing assignments, how much cognitive scaffolding we build into every lesson plan, or how much we tell students what to do with their papers versus letting them do some of the crucial cognitive heavy-lifting. The nuances of this pedagogical balancing act are brought especially to light when students and teachers in writing classrooms and tutors from the writing center or other tutoring programs are brought together under what Neal Lerner characterizes as the "big cross-disciplinary tent" of peer-to-peer teaching and learning (qtd. in Fitzgerald 73). Like many teachers of writing, I started my career under this expansive tent learning to negotiate directive and nondirective instruction with students from across cultures and across the disciplines.

I started out as a tutor at Edmonds Community College (near Seattle, Washington) in 1997. When I made my way as a GTA teaching my own section of first-year composition at the University of Washington, in 2002, I took my writing-centered attitudes and methods right along with me. My initial problem was how to make the classroom more like the center I felt so strongly served students in more individualized and interpersonal ways. I began to ask the question: Can I make every writing classroom (as much as possible) a "writing center"? Luckily, I soon found out I was not alone in this quest for pedagogical synergy. Curriculum- and classroom-based tutoring offer exciting, dramatic instructional arenas from which to continue asking questions and provoking conversations involving closer classroom and writing center/tutoring connections (Spigelman and Grobman; Moss, Highberg, and Nicolas; Soven; Lutes; Zawacki; Hall and Hughes; Cairns and Anderson; Corbett "Bringing," "Using," "Negotiating"). In the Introduction to *On Location: Theory and Practice in Classroom-Based Writing Tutoring* Candace Spigelman and Laurie Grobman differentiate between the more familiar *curriculum-based tutoring*, usually associated with writing fellows programs, and *classroom-based tutoring*, where tutorial support is offered during class (often in developmental writing courses). But just as all writing centers are not alike, both curriculum- and classroom-based tutoring programs differ from institution to institution. There is much variation involved in curriculum- and classroom-based tutoring due to the context-specific needs and desires of students, tutors, instructors, and program administrators: Some programs ask tutors to comment on student papers; some programs make visits to tutors optional, while others make them mandatory; some have tutors attend class as often as possible, while others do not; and some programs offer various hybrid approaches. Due to the considerable overlap in theory and practice between curriculum- and classroom-based tutoring, I have opted for the term *course-based tutoring* (still CBT) when referring to pedagogical elements shared by both.

The following quotes, from three of the case-study participants this book reports on, begin to suggest the types of teaching and learning choices afforded by CBT, especially for developmental teachers and learners:

> I feel like when I'm in the writing center just doing individual sign up appointments it's much more transient. People come and you don't see them and you don't hear from them until they show up and they have their paper with them and it's the first time you see them, the first time you see their work, and you go through and you help them and then they leave. And whether they come back or not it's up to them but you're not really as tied to them. And I felt more tied to the success of the students in this class. I really wanted them to do better.
>
> – Sam, course-based tutor

> One of the best features of my introductory English course was the built-in support system that was available to me. It was a small class, and my professor was able to give all of us individual assistance. In addition, the class had a peer tutor who was always available to help me. My tutor helped alleviate my anxiety over the understanding of assignments as she would go over the specifics with me before I started it

> ... When I did not understand something, my professor and tutor would patiently explain the material to me. My fears lessened as my confidence grew and I took more chances with my writing, which was a big step for me.
>
> – Max, first-year developmental writer

> I'd be interested in seeing how having a tutor in my class all the time would work, but at the same time one of the things I'm afraid of is that the tutor would know all the readings that we're doing and would know the kinds of arguments I'm looking for and they might steer the students in that direction instead of giving that other point of view that I'm hoping they get from the tutor.
>
> – Sarah, graduate writing instructor

We hear the voice of a course-based tutor at the University of Washington (UW), Sam, reflecting on her experiences working more closely with developmental writers in one course. We feel her heightened sense of commitment to these students, her desire to help them succeed in that particular course. We will hear much more about Sam's experiences in Chapter Three. We also hear the voice of a developmental writer from Southern Connecticut State University (SCSU), Max, a student with autism who worked closely with a course-based tutor. Max intimates how his peer tutor acted much like an assistant or associate teacher for the course. He suggests how this tutor earned his *trust* and boosted his confidence, helping to provide a warm and supportive learning environment conducive to preparing him for the rigors of academic writing and communication. And, in the third quote, we hear from a graduate student and course instructor at the University of Washington, Sarah, who expresses her concern for having a tutor too "in the know" and how that more intimate knowledge of her expectations might affect the student writer/tutor interaction. We will hear much more from student teachers like Sarah (as well as more experienced classroom instructors) especially in Chapters Three and Four. Experiences like the ones hinted at by these three diverse students (at very different levels) deserve closer listening for what they have to teach us all, whether we feel more at home in the writing center or writing classroom.

ANSWERING EXIGENCIES FROM THE FIELD(S)

While enough has been written on this topic to establish some theoretical and practical starting points for research, currently there are two major avenues that warrant generative investigation. First, although many CBT programs include one-to-one and group tutorials, there are few studies on the effects of participant interactions on these tutorials (Bruland; Corbett "Using"; and Mackiewicz and Thompson being notable exceptions). And only two (Corbett, "Using"; Mackiewicz and Thompson, Chapter 8) provide transcript reporting and analyses of the tutorials that frequently occur outside of the classroom. Valuable linguistic and rhetorical evidence that bring us closer to an understanding and appreciation of the dynamics of course-based tutoring—*and* peer-to-peer teaching and learning—can be gained from systematically analyzing what tutorial transcripts have to offer. Second, is the need for research on the effects of CBT with multicultural and nonmainstream students (see Spigelman and Grobman, 227-30). CBT provides the potential means for extending the type of dialogic, multiple-perspectival interaction in the developmental classroom scholars in collections like *Academic Literacy in the English Classroom, Writing in Multicultural Settings, Bakhtinian Perspectives on Language, Literacy, and Learning,* and *Diversity in the Composition Classroom* encourage—though not without practical and theoretical drama and complications.

Beyond Dichotomy begins to answer both these needs with multi-method qualitative case studies of CBT and one-to-one conferences in multiple sections of developmental first-year composition at two universities—a large, west coast R1 (the University of Washington, Seattle) and a medium, east coast master's (Southern Connecticut State University, New Haven). These studies use a combination of rhetorical and discourse analyses and ethnographic and case-study methods to investigate both the scenes of teaching and learning in CBT, as well as the points of view and interpretations of all the participating actors in these scenes—instructors, peer tutors, students, and researcher/program administrator.

This book extends the research on CBT—and the important implications for peer-to-peer learning and one-to-one tutoring and conferencing—by examining the much-needed rhetorical and linguistic connections between what goes on in classroom interactions, planning, and one-to-one tutorials from multiple methodological and analytical angles and interpretive points of view. If we are to continue historicizing, theorizing, and building synergistic partnerships between writing classrooms and the peer tutoring programs that support them, we should have a deeper understanding of the wide array of choices—both methodological and interpersonal—that practitioners have, as well as more nuanced methods for analyzing the rhetorical and linguistic forces and features that can enable or deter closer instructional partnerships. This study ultimately presents pedagogical and methodological conclusions and implications usable for educators looking to build and sustain stronger pedagogical bridges between peer tutoring programs and writing classrooms: from classroom instructors and program administrators in Composition and Rhetoric, to writing center, writing fellows, supplemental instruction, and WAC/WID theorists and practitioners.

The lessons whispered by the participants in this book's studies echo with pedagogical implications. For teaching one-to-one, what might Sam's thoughts quoted above about being "more tied to the success of the students" or Sarah's intimations regarding a tutor being more directly attached to her course add to conversations involving directive/nondirective instruction and teacher/tutor role negotiation? What might Max's sentiments regarding writing anxiety—and how the pedagogical teamwork of his instructor and tutor in his developmental writing course helped him cope—contribute to our understanding of what pedagogical strategies tutors and teachers might deploy with struggling first-year students? In short, what are teachers, tutors, and student writers getting out of these experiences, and what effects do these interactions have on tutor and teacher instructional choices and identity formations? An important and related question for the arguments in this book, then, becomes how soon can developing/developmental student writers, potential writing tutors, and classroom instructors or teaching assistants be involved in the authoritative, socially, and personally complicated acts of collaborative peer-to-peer teaching and learning? When are they ready to model those coveted *Framework for Success in Postsecondary Writing* "habits of mind essential for success in college writing?" When are they ready to balance between strategically directing thought and action and holding back when coaching peers to become more habitually curious, open, engaged, creative, persistent, responsible, flexible, and metacognitive? There are important pedagogical connections between how and with whom these habits of mind are fostered and how students develop as college writers (see, for example, Thaiss and Zawacki; Beaufort; Carroll) that studies in CBT can bring into high relief. In sum, this book will explore, elaborate on, and provide some answers to the following central question: How can what we know about peer tutoring one-to-one and in small groups—especially the implications of directive and nondirective tutoring strategies and methods brought to light in this book—inform our work with students in writing centers and other tutoring programs, as well as in writing classrooms? I'll start this investigation by looking at why we should continue to build bridges that synergistically bring writing classrooms and tutoring programs closer together.

RECLAIMING THE WRITING CLASSROOM INTO "THE IDEA OF A WRITING CENTER"

Above we discussed the exigencies for this book's case studies. But bridging and synergizing the best of writing center and writing classroom pedagogies could be considered the uber-exigency that gave birth to CBT programs in the first place. In his pivotal 1984 *College English* essay, Stephen North passionately let loose the frustrations many writing center practitioners felt about centers being seen as proofreading, or grammar fix-it shops, or as otherwise subservient to the writing classroom. In this polemical "declaration of independence," North spelled out a, thereafter, much-repeated idea that writing tutors are concerned with producing better writers not necessarily better writing. North's emphasis on writers' processes over products, his insistence that the interpersonal talk that foregrounds and surrounds the one-to-one tutorial is what makes writing centers uniquely positioned to offer something lacking in typical classroom instruction (including the notion that tutors are not saddled with the responsibility of institutional judger-grader), touched on foundational writing center ideology. But North's vehemence would also draw a theoretical and practical dividing line between "we" in the center and "them" in the classroom as well as a host of critiques and counterstatements (North "Revisting"; Smith; Hemmeter; Smulyan and Bolton; Healy; Raines; Soliday "Shifting"; Boquet and Lerner). Further, this divisive attitude may have also contributed to the self-imposed marginalization of the writing center in relation to the rest of the academy, as Jane Nelson and Margaret Garner—in their analyses of the University of Wyoming Writing Center's history under John and Tilly Warnock—claim occurred in the 1970s and 1980s. The trend for arguing from a perspective of what we *can't* or *won't* do was stubbornly set.

Though encouraging more of a two-way street between classroom and center, Dave Healy, Mary Soliday ("Shifting"), Teagan Decker, and Margot Soven have all drawn on Harvey Kail and John Trimbur's 1987 essay "The Politics of Peer Tutoring" to remind us that the center is often that place just removed enough from the power structures of the classroom to enable students to engage in critical questioning of the "seemingly untouchable expectations, goals and motivations of the power structures" that undergraduates must learn within (Decker, "Diplomatic" 22). In another 1987 essay, Trimbur, drawing on Kenneth Bruffee's notion of "little teachers," warned practitioners of the problem of treating peer tutors as para- or pre-professionals and to recognize "that their community is not necessarily ours" (294). Bruffee and Trimbur worry that the collaborative effect of peership, or the positive effects of working closer perhaps to the student's Vygotsykyan zone of proximal development, will be lost if tutors are trained to be too teacherly. Muriel Harris intimates, in her 2001 "Centering in on Professional Choices," her own personal and professional reasons for why she prefers writing center tutoring and administration over classroom instruction. Commenting on her experience as an instructor teaching writing in the classroom, she opines: "Several semesters passed as I became ever more uneasy with grading disembodied, faceless papers, standing in front of large classes trying to engage everyone in meaningful group discussions, and realizing that I wasn't making contact in truly useful ways with each student as a writer composing text" (431). She views her experiences in writing centers, in contrast, as enabling her to focus on "the copious differences and endless varieties among writers and ways to uncover those individualities and use that knowledge when interacting with each writer" (433). And there it is again, the scapegoat doing its potentially divisive work via one of the most influential voices in teaching one-to-one and peer-to-peer. Those of us theorizing, practicing, and advocating CBT, then, must stay wary of the sorts of power, authority, and methodological issues that might potentially undermine important pedagogical aspects of the traditional one-to-one tutorial. These same issues of authority—which touch importantly on concepts like trust-building and directive/nondirective tutoring—come into play as we look to the various "parent genres" that inform the theory and practice of the instructional hybrid that is CBT: writing center tutoring, WAC writing fellows programs, peer writing groups, and supplemental instruction (Figure 1).

THE PROTEAN STATE OF THE FIELD IN COURSE-BASED WRITING TUTORING

As Spigelman and Grobman describe in their Introduction to *On Location,* the strength—and concurrent complexity—of CBT lies in large part to the variety of instructional support systems that can constitute its theory and practice, the way these instructional genres mix and begin to blur as they are called upon in different settings and by different participants to form the instructional hybrid that is CBT. The authors draw on Charles Bazerman and Anis Bawarshi to expand the notion of genre from purely a means of textual categorization to a metaphorical conceptualization of genre as *location.* In Bazerman's terms genres are "environments for learning. They are locations within which meaning is constructed" (qtd. in Spigelman and Grobman 2). For Bawarshi, "genres do not just help us define and organize texts; they also help us define and organize kinds of situations and social actions, situations and actions that the genres, through their use, rhetorically make possible" (qtd. in Spigelman and Grobman 2). Rather than practice in the center, or in the classroom, rather than seeing teacher here and tutor there and student over there, CBT asks all participants in the dynamic drama of teaching and learning to realize as fully as possible the myriad possible means of connecting. For CBT, genre as location opens to the imagination visions of communicative roads interconnecting locations, commu-

Figure 1: The parent genres that inform CBT.

nication roads that can be free-flowing or grindingly congested, locations where people inhabit spaces and make rhetorical and discursive moves in sometimes smooth, sometimes frictional ways. For Spigelman and Grobman, this leads to two significant features: a new generic form emerges from this generic blending, "but it also enacts the *play of differences* among those parent features" (4; emphasis added). This generic play of differences—between parent forms, between participants acting within and upon this ever-blurring, context-based instructional practice—makes CBT such a compelling location for continued rhetorical and pedagogical investigation.

Pragmatics begin to blend with possibilities as we begin to ask what might be. What can we learn from CBT theory and practice that can help us build more synergistic pedagogies in our programs, for our colleagues, with our students? Furthering Spigelman and Grobman's idea of the play of differences, by critiquing the smaller instructional genres (themselves, already complex), readers will begin to gain an intimate sense of the choices involved in the design of protean, hybrid CBT programs and initiatives. This break-down of the parent instructional genres will also provide further background of the many ways practitioners have strived to forge connections between writing classrooms and writing support systems discussed above, and begin to suggest pedagogical complications like directive/nondirective instruction in the theory and practice of CBT.

Writing Center Tutoring

Writing center tutoring is the most obvious, influential parent genre to start with. Harris, Bruffee, and North have pointed to perhaps the key ingredients that make writing center tutorials an important part of a writing curriculum. Harris has helped many compositionists see that the professional choice of doing or supporting writing center work can add much to both students' and teachers' understanding of how writers think and learn. Harris claims, "When meeting with tutors, writers gain the kinds of knowledge about their writing and about themselves that are not possible in other institutional settings" ("Talking" 27). Bruffee similarly makes grand assertions for the role of peer tutoring in institutional change. Bruffee contends peer tutors have the ability, through conversation, to translate at the boundaries between the knowledge communities students belong to and the knowledge communities they aspire to join. Students will internalize this conversation of the community they want to join so they can call on it on their own. This mediating role, he believes, can bring about "changes in the prevailing understanding of the nature and authority of knowledge and the authority of teachers" (*Collaborative Learning* 110). But this theoretical idea of the ground-shaking institutional change that can be brought about by peer tutoring runs into some practical problems when we consider such dimensions as subject matter expertise, personality, attitude, and just how deeply entrenched the power and authority of the classroom instructor really is. A tutor snug, even smug and secure in his or her belief that they are challenging "the prevailing understanding" and authority of the teacher or institution in one-to-ones may be naively misconstruing the complex nature of what it means to teach a number of individuals, with a number of individual learning styles and competencies, in the writing classroom. Often the voices of hierarchical authority ring loud in tutors' and students' ears, understandably transcending all other motives during instructional and learning acts.

Tutors and instructors involved in CBT instructional situations bring their own internalized versions of the "conversations of the communities" they belong to or aspire to join. Some tutors, for example, bring what they have come to understand or believe as the role of a tutor—often imagined as a nondirective, non-authoritarian peer—into classroom situations where students may have internalized a different set of assumptions or beliefs of how instruction should function in order for them to join the sorts of communities *they* aspire to join. Instructors, in turn, may look to tutors to be more hands-on and directive or more minimalist and traditionally peer-like, often causing authority and role confusion between everyone involved. Bruffee compounds this dilemma of tutor authority with his view of the mediating *role* of peer tutors. In support of his antifoundational argument for education, in the second edition of *Collaborative Learning*, Bruffee distinguishes between two forms of peer tutoring programs: monitoring and collaborative. In the monitoring model, tutors "are select, superior students who for all intents and purposes serve as faculty surrogates under faculty supervision. Their peer status is so thoroughly compromised that they are educationally effective only in strictly traditional academic terms" (97). In contrast, Bruffee argues that collaborative tutors: "do not mediate directly between tutees and their teachers" (97); they do not explicitly instruct as teachers do, but rather "guide and support" tutees to help them "translate at the boundaries between the knowledge communities they already belong to and the knowledge communities they aspire to join" (98). Bruffee, however, does acknowledge the fact that no collaborative tutoring program is completely uncompromised by issues of trust and authority, just as no monitoring program consists only of "little teacher" clones.

As we will see in the following sections—and throughout this book—the issues raised by Harris and Bruffee become increasingly multifaceted as social actors play on their notions of what it means to tutor, teach, and learn writing in and outside of the classroom. In CBT situations, the task of assignment translation can take a different turn when tutors have insider knowledge of teacher expectations. The affective or motivational dimension, often so important in tutoring or in the classroom (especially in nonmainstream settings), can either be strengthened or diminished in CBT. And the question of tutor authority, whether more "tutorly" or "teacherly" approaches make for better one-to-one or small-group interactions, begins to branch into ever-winding streams of qualification.

WAC Writing Fellows

This idea of just how and to what degree peer tutoring might affect the power dynamics of the classroom leads us straight into considerations of writing fellows programs. The fact that writing fellows usually comment on student drafts of papers and then meet one-to-one with students, sometimes without even attending class or even doing the same readings as the students (as with Team

Four detailed in this book), points immediately to issues of power, authority, and tutor-tutee-teacher trust-building relationships relevant for CBT. The role of the writing fellow also raises the closely related issue of directive/nondirective approaches to peer tutoring. These theoretical and practical challenges hold special relevance for writing fellows (Haring-Smith). While Margot Soven commented on such logistical issues as students committing necessary time, carelessly written student drafts, and issues of time and place in meetings in 1993, the issue most practitioners currently fret over falls along the lines of instructional identity, of pedagogical authority and directiveness. Who and what is a writing fellow supposed to be?

Several writing fellows practitioners report on compelling conflicts during the vagaries of authority and method negotiation (Lutes; Zawacki; Severino and Trachsel; Corroy; Babcock and Thonus 75-77; Corbett "Using," "Negotiating"). Jean Marie Lutes examines a reflective essay written by a University of Wisconsin, Madison fellow in which the fellow, Jill, describes an instance of being accosted by another fellow for "helping an oppressive academy to stifle a student's creative voice" (243). Jill defends her role as peer tutor just trying to pass on a repertoire of strategies and skills that would foster her peer's creativity. Lutes goes on to argue that in their role as writing fellows, tutors are more concerned with living up to the role of "ideal tutor" than whether or not they have become complicit in an institutional system of rigid conventional indoctrination. In an instance of the controlling force of better knowing the professor's goals in one-to-one interactions, another fellow, Helen, reports how she resorted to a more directive style of tutoring when she noticed students getting closer to the professor's expectations. Helen concluded that this more intimate knowledge of the professor's expectations, once she "knew the answer" (250 n.18) made her job harder rather than easier to negotiate. The sorts of give and take surrounding CBT negotiations, the intellectual and social pressures it exerts on tutors, leads Lutes to ultimately argue that "the [writing fellows] program complicates the peer relationship between fellows and students; when fellows comment on drafts, they inevitably write not only for their immediate audience (the student writers), but also for their future audience (the professor)" (239).

Clearly, as these cases report, the issue of changing classroom teaching practices and philosophies (to say nothing of institutional change) is difficult to qualify. It places tutors in a double-bind: The closer understanding of teacher expectations, as Bruffee warned, can cause tutors to feel obligated to share what they know, moving them further away from "peer" status. If they don't, they may feel as if they are withholding valuable information from tutees, and the tutees may feel the same way, again moving tutors further away from peer status. Yet Mary Soliday illustrates ways this tension can be put to productive use. In *Every-*

day Genres she describes the writing fellows program at the City College of New York in terms of how the collaborations she studied led professors to design and implement improved assignments in their courses. One of the keys to the success of the program, Soliday claims, involves the apprenticeship model, wherein new fellows are paired with veteran fellows for their first semester. Only after experiencing a substantial amount of time watching their mentors interact with professors—witnessing their mentors trying to grasp the purposes and motives of their professorial partners—were these WAC apprentices ready to face the complexities of negotiating pedagogical authority themselves (also see Robinson and Hall). Cautionary tales (like the ones presented in Chapters Three and Four of this book) have also led writing fellow practitioners to attempt to devise some rules of thumb for best practices. Emily Hall and Bradley Hughes, in "Preparing Faculty, Professionalizing Fellows," report on the same sorts of conflict in authority and trust discussed above with Lutes. They go on to detail the why's and how's of training and preparing both faculty and fellows for closer instructional partnerships, including a quote intimated by a fellow that he or she was trained in "a non-directive conferencing style" (32).

But what, exactly, are the features of a "nondirective" conferencing style? Is it something that can be pinpointed and mapped? Is it something that can be learned and taught? And, importantly for this study, what useful connections might be drawn between directive/nondirective one-to-one tutoring and small-group peer response and other classroom-based activities?

Peer Writing Groups

And the pedagogical inter-issues don't get any less complicated as we turn now to writing groups—what I view as the crucial intersection between writing center, peer tutoring, and classroom pedagogies central to CBT. Influenced by the work of Bruffee, Donald Murray, Peter Elbow, Linda Flower and John Hayes, Anne Ruggles Gere, and Ann Berthoff, in *Small Groups in Writing Workshops* Robert Brooke, Ruth Mirtz, and Rick Evans attempted to illustrate how students learn the rules of written language in similar ways to how growing children learn oral language—through intensive interaction with both oral and written conversations with their peers and teachers. Marie Nelson's work, soon after to be deemed the "studio" approach in the work of Rhonda Grego and Nancy Thompson, provides case studies that supported Brooke, Mirtz, and Evans's claims with compelling empirical evidence. For example, and especially pertinent to the case studies reported on in this book in Chapter Four, Nelson's study of some 90 developmental and multicultural response groups identified consistent patterns of salutary development in students learning to write and instructors learning to teach. Student writers usually moved in an overwhelmingly predictable pattern from dependence on instructor authority, to interdependence on their fellow group members, ultimately to an internalized independence, confidence and trust in their own abilities (that they could then re-externalize for the benefit of their group mates). Nelson noted that this pattern was accompanied by, and substantially expedited when, the pedagogical attitudes and actions of the TA group facilitators started off more directive in their instruction and gradually relinquished instructional control (for a smaller, 2008, case study that supports Nelson's findings see Launspach).

But as fast as scholars could publish their arguments urging the use of peer response groups, others began to question this somewhat pretty picture of collaboration. Donald Stewart, drawing on Isabel Briggs Myers, argued that people with different personality types will have more trouble collaborating well with each other. Brooke, Mirtz, and Evans, while ultimately arguing for the benefits of writing groups, also described potential drawbacks like students negotiating sensitive private/public writing issues with others, reconciling interdependent writing situations with other writing teachers and classes they've experienced that did not value peer-to-peer collaborative learning, or working with diverse peers or peers unlike themselves. In her 1992 "Collaboration Is Not Collaboration Is Not Collaboration" Harris, focusing on issues like experience and confidence, compares peer response groups and peer tutoring. She explains how tutoring offers the kind of individualized, nonjudgmental focus lacking in the classroom, while peer response is done in closer proximity to course guidelines and with practice in working with a variety of reviewers. She also raises some concerns. One problem involves how students might evaluate each other's writing with a different set of standards than their teachers: "Students may likely be reinforcing each other's abilities to write discourse for their peers, not for the academy—a sticky problem indeed, especially when teachers suggest that an appropriate audience for a particular paper might be the class itself" (379). Fifteen years later, Eric Paulson, Jonathan Alexander, and Sonya Armstrong report on a peer response study of fifteen first-year students. The researchers used eye-tracking software to study what students spend time on while reading and responding. The authors found that students spend much more time focused on later-order concerns (LOCs) like grammar and spelling than higher-order concerns (HOCs) like claim and organization, and were hesitant to provide detailed critique. While their study can be criticized due to the fact that the students in the study were responding to an outside text rather than a peer group member's text, and none of the students had any training or experience in peer response, the findings echo Harris's concerns regarding students' abilities to provide useful response. Obviously, the issue here is student authority and confidence. If students have not been trained in the arts of peer response, how can they be expected to give adequate response when put into groups, especially if the student is a first-year or an otherwise inexperienced academic reader and writer? How can we help "our students experience and reap the benefits of both forms of collaboration?" Harris is curious to know (381).

Writing center and peer tutoring programs from Penn State at Berks, UW at Seattle, University of Connecticut at Storrs, and Southern Illinois University at Carbondale, among many others, have answered Wendy Bishop's call from 1988 to be "willing to experiment" (124) with peer response group work. Tutors have been sent into classrooms to help move students toward meta-awareness of how to tutor each other. In effect, they become tutor trainers, coaching fellow students on strategies to employ while responding to a peer's paper. But student anxiety around issues of plagiarism and autonomous originality are hard to dispel. Spigelman suggests that students need to know how the collaborative generation of ideas differs from plagiarism. If students can understand how and why authors appropriate ideas, they may be more willing to experiment with collaborative writing ("Ethics"). It follows, then, that tutors, who are adept at these collaborative writing negotiations, can direct fellow students toward understanding the difference. But as with all the issues we've been exploring so far, the issue of the appropriation of ideas is as Harris suggests a sticky one indeed. In another essay Spigelman, drawing on Nancy Grimm and Andrea Lunsford, comments on the desires of basic writers interacting with peer group leaders who look to the tutor as surrogate teacher ("Reconstructing"). She relates that no matter how hard the tutors tried to displace their roles as authority figures, the basic writers inevitably complained about not getting enough grammar instruction, or lack of explicit directions. While on the other hand, when a tutor tried to be more directive and teacherly, students resisted her efforts at control as well. Spigelman also relates how she experiences similar reactions from students. Her accounts, as with Lutes above, suggest that it is no easy task experimenting with and working toward restructuring authority in the writing classroom.

In the 2014 collection *Peer Pressure, Peer Power: Theory and Practice in Peer Review and Response for the Writing Classroom* (Corbett, LaFrance, and Decker) several essays attempt to provide answers to the authority and methods questions Harris and Spigelman raise. One of the recurring themes in the collection is the reevaluated role of the instructor in coaching peer review and response groups. Contributors like Kory Ching and Chris Gerben illustrate how instructors can take an active (directive) role in coaching students how to coach each other in small-group response sessions by actively modeling useful response strategies (also see Hoover). Ellen Carillo uses blogs and online discussions to encourage student conversation and collaborative critical thinking as an inventive, generative form of peer response. Carillo encourages students to question the nature of collaboration and to become more aware of the ways authors ethically participate in conversation as a form of inquiry. And Harris herself, in her afterword to the collection, offers in essence a revisit to her "Collaboration" essay. Like several other authors in the collection, Harris draws on writing center theory and practice, combined with classroom peer response practice, to speculate on how we just might be making some strides in working toward viable writing-center-inspired strategies for successful peer-to-peer reciprocal teaching and learning in writing classrooms. Ultimately, Harris's summation of the collection, and her thoughtful extensions and suggestions, argue for a huge amount of preparation, practice, and follow-up when trying to make peer response groups work well, suggesting as E. Shelley Reid does, that perhaps peer review and response is the most promising collaborative practice we can deploy in the writing classroom. Harris realizes there are multiple ways of reaching this goal: "Whatever the path to getting students to recognize on their own that that they are going to have the opportunity to become more skilled writers, the goal—to help students see the value of peer review before they begin and then to actively engage in it—is the same" (281). Harris makes it clear that she believes a true team effort is involved in this process of getting students to collaboratively internalize (and externalize) the value of peer response, an effort that must actively involve student writers, instructors, and—as often as possible—peer tutors.

It is important that those practicing peer review and response come to understand just how useful the intellectual and social skills exercised and developed—through the reciprocity between reader/writer, tutor/student writer, tutor/instructor—really can be. Isabel Thompson et al. agree with Harris's sentiments in their call for studies that compare and contrast the language of writing groups to the language of one-to-one tutorials. This line of inquiry would be especially useful for CBT, since tutors are often involved in working with student writers in peer response groups, usually in the classroom. I attempt exactly this sort of comparative analyses in Chapters Two, Three, and Four.

Supplemental Instruction

The final branch of peer education we will look at, supplemental instruction (SI), is given the least amount of coverage in peer education literature, though it purports to serve a quarter million students across the country each academic term (Arendale). SI draws theoretically from learning theory in cognitive and developmental educational psychology. There are four key participants in the SI program, the SI leader, the SI supervisor, the students, and the faculty instructor. The SI leader attends training before classes start, attends the targeted classes, takes notes, does homework, and reads all assigned materials. Leaders conduct at least three to five SI sessions each week, choose and employ appropriate session strategies, support faculty, meet with their SI supervisor regularly, and assist their SI supervisor in training other SI leaders (Hurley, Jacobs, and Gilbert). SI leaders work to help students break down complex information into smaller parts; they try to help students see the cause/effect relationship between study habits and strategies and resulting performances; and because they are often in the same class each day, and doing the same work as the student, they need to be good performance models. SI leaders try to help students use prior knowledge to help learn new knowledge, and encourage cognitive conflict by pointing out problems in their understandings of information (Hurley, Jacobs, and Gilbert; Ender and Newton). In this sense, supplemental instruction also demands that SI leaders, much like tutors, must negotiate when to be more directive or nondirective in their pedagogical support.

Spigelman and Grobman report on the links between supplemental instruction and composition courses. Drawing on the work of Gary Hafer, they write: "Hafer argues that it is a common misperception that one-to-one tutoring works better than SI in composition courses, which are not identified as high-risk courses and which are thought by those outside the discipline to be void of 'content'" (236). In Hafer's view, the goals of SI have more in common with collaborative composition pedagogy than do one-to-one tutorials in the writing center. These choices between what one-to-ones are offering versus what other potential benefits may present themselves with other peer tutoring models make for interesting comparative considerations and potential instructional choices. Several of the case studies I've been involved in over the years, including ones reported on in this book, incorporate several prominent features of the SI model, including tutors attending class on a daily basis, doing the course readings, and meeting with student writers outside of class. (For more on SI, visit the website for the International Center for SI housed at the University of Missouri at Kansas City.)

The rest of this book sets up and presents case studies of my experimentation over the years with hybridizing these parent genres that make up CBT. I illustrate the many ups and downs of diverse people with different personalities and views of "best practices" in teaching and learning to write trying to get along, trying to understand how they might best contribute to a synergistic instructional partnership while attempting to realize the best ways to impart the most useful knowledge to developing student writers. Synergy (from the ancient Greek *synergia* or *syn-* "together" and *ergon* "work") involves identifying the best of what each contributing collaborator has to offer. As we've been touching on, one of the most crucial considerations tutors—indeed any teacher—must face in any instructional situation is the issue of how directive versus how nondirective they can, should or choose to be and, importantly, how this intertwines with the issue of authority and trust negotiation. Kenneth Burke writes, "we might well keep in mind that a speaker persuades an audience by the use of stylistic identifications ... So, there is no chance of our keeping apart the meanings of persuasion, identification ('consubstantiality') and communication (the nature of rhetoric as 'addressed')" (*Rhetoric* 46). This book aims to focus our attention on the importance of these interpersonal "stylistic identifications," urging teachers and tutors to consider the true balancing act demanded by the directive/nondirective pedagogical continuum.

CHAPTER SUMMARIES

Chapter One, takes a careful look at the ongoing rhetoric of directive and nondirective tutoring strategies. This issue has a long history in writing center literature, and it brings us to the heart of some of one-to-one teachers' most closely-held beliefs and practices. I examine the conflict inherent when tutors are brought into the tighter instructional orbit that is CBT and how practitioners have dealt with thorny issues of instructional authority and role negotiation when moving between center and classroom. Carefully analyzing the literature on peer tutoring, I argue that CBT contexts demand a close reconsideration of our typically nondirective, hands-off approach to tutoring, that tutors involved in CBT, especially with developmental students, can better serve (and *be* better served) if they are encouraged to broaden their instructional repertoires, if directors and coordinators cultivate a more flexible notion of what it means to tutor in the writing center, in the classroom, and in between. I begin exploring, however, the complications involved in this idealistic notion of instructional flexibility.

Chapter Two offers the multi-method, RAD-research case study methods and methodology employed in Chapters Three and Four. I begin to offer some of the back-story on the dramatic effects the widely varying level of interaction in and out of the classroom—as well as variables like tutor experience, training, identity, and personality—ended up having on participants' actions in and perceptions of their CBT experiences. I detail methods of analyses for one-to-one tutorials for Chapter Three and peer response groups in Chapter Four.

Chapter Three presents and analyzes the one-to-one tutorials that occurred with four teams from the UW. Audio-recorded one-to-one transcripts are the central focus of analysis used to explore the question: What rhetorical and linguistic patterns surface during one-to-one tutorials, and what relationship (if any) do participant interactions and various CBT contexts have on these one-to-ones? I carefully analyze how the discourse features of tutorial transcripts such as number of words spoken, references to instructors and assignment prompts, overlaps, discourse markers, pauses and silences, and qualifiers hint at larger rhetorical issues involved in the drama of closer collaboration. I attempt to triangulate and enrich these linguistic analyses comparatively with the points of view of participants.

Chapter Four provides the findings and analysis of CBT partnerships from the UW and SCSU engaged in small-group peer review and response facilitation and other classroom interactions. While field notes from in-class observations offer my views, I also present interviews and journal excerpts from the participants and report on feedback from students to provide more perspectives on these interactions. This chapter points to some illuminating findings that, when compared to the studies of one-to-one tutorials from the UW, offer readers an intimate look at the myriad choices practitioners have with CBT—and the teaching and learning implications involved for all participants.

In the *Conclusion* I discuss implications of this study's findings in relation to my primary research question: How can what we know about peer tutoring one-to-one and in small groups—especially the implications of directive and nondirective tutoring strategies and methods—inform our work with students in writing centers and other tutoring programs, as well as classrooms? I begin with the implications of how this question played out in all aspects of the case studies, from the participants' points of view, to the one-to-one tutorial transcript analyses and interpretations, and finally to the peer response sessions and other classroom activities I observed and followed up on. Finally, I open the conclusion to implications for tutor education and development, program building, and I suggest choices for teaching, learning and researching writing including interconnections between one-to-one and small-group teaching and learning.

CHAPTER ONE

TUTORING STYLE, TUTORING STRATEGY: COURSE-BASED TUTORING AND THE HISTORY, RHETORIC, AND REALITY OF THE DIRECTIVE/NONDIRECTIVE INSTRUCTIONAL CONTINUUM

> I don't want students to perceive me as having all the answers, yet very often I do have the answers they are looking for, and the students themselves know it ... What sort of message are we sending to the students we tutor if they perceive us as withholding information vital to their academic success?
>
> – Elizabeth Boquet, "Intellectual Tug-of-War"

> Familiar memes—don't write on the paper, don't speak more than the student-writer, ask non-directive questions—get passed among cohorts of writing tutors as gospel before they even interact with writers in an everyday setting.
>
> – Anne Ellen Geller, Michele Eodice, Frankie Condon, Meg Carroll, and Elizabeth Boquet

Arguably, no single issue in writing center and peer tutoring theory and practice gets at the heart of one-to-one, small group, or classroom instruction as the question of directive/nondirective teaching methods. The question of how and when tutors (or instructors) should use techniques like open-ended ("Socratic") questioning versus just telling students what they think they should do, or what the tutor might do themselves if they were in the tutee's position, raises issues involving tutor authority, tutor-tutee (and even instructor) trust, tutor training (or "tutor education" or "apprenticing"), and writing process versus product—all relevant concerns in any writing instruction situation. However, when the rhetorical situation of typical one-to-one tutoring changes—when tutors, students, and instructors are brought into tighter instructional orbits—so too must typical instructional methods and styles be reconsidered. Further, add into the equation the fact that student writers, tutors, and instructors might have various levels of experience, preparation, and personality and things get even more dramatically complicated. This is the case in situations involving the closer collaboration of CBT programs. How can tutors and tutor coaches (directors, coordinators) adjust their typical tutoring and tutor training styles and methods to accommodate these sorts of multifaceted rhetorical situations?

In their 2008 *College English* essay, Elizabeth Boquet and Neal Lerner draw on critiques of Stephen North to argue that we need to be more open to experiencing two-way streets in theory, research, and practice—in short, instructional learning—between writing classrooms and writing centers. Lerner argues further in his 2009 *The Idea of a Writing Laboratory* that writing centers can be much more than physical places or removed sites for tutoring. Writing center theory and practice can branch out into many methods and forms for pedagogical experimentation. He writes, "Rather than a classroom teacher acting as expert witness, jury, and judge in evaluation of students' writing, writing centers have long offered themselves as nonevaluative, relatively safe places, as *experiments* in the teaching of writing" (15). But what happens when a tutor travels from that relatively "safe" center to the forbidding land of the "expert" classroom teacher? My experimental research and practice on CBT since 2000 has led me to important questions this chapter addresses: How and in what ways can what we know about the rhetoric of peer tutoring styles and methods from writing fellows, supplemental instruction, writing groups, and teaching one-to-one be applied and studied. Then how and why might we share these finding with all teachers of writing? The rhetoric of the directive/nondirective instructional continuum—so often debated, refined, and even resisted in writing center and other peer tutoring circles—offers much in terms of teaching philosophy, holds great practical and critical promise, and needs to be shared with all teachers of writing. In many ways, the focus on how participants negotiate the directive/nondirective continuum offers immense teaching, learning, and communicative implications. Like Harry Denny, I am interested not only in the pragmatics of peer-to-peer teaching and learning, but what these pragmatics might reveal in terms of the bodies (minds) and politics of the various social actors in these collaborative learning ecologies. How and why can purposefully withholding knowledge from a student—in order to activate their own critical and creative powers—affect the teaching-learning dynamic? When and in what ways can simply telling students or tutors what they should or must do be more or less beneficial?

Much has been written on the nondirective or minimalist tutoring approach (see, for example, Ashton-Jones; Brooks; Harris, *Teaching One-to-One*) and subsequent critiques of this approach (see Clark "Collaboration," "Perspectives"; Clark and Healy; Shamoon and Burns; Grimm; Boquet "Intellectual," *Noise*; Carino; Geller et al.; Corbett, "Tutoring," "Negotiating"; compare to Gillespie and Lerner's notion of control/flexibility). I will begin by analyzing several key texts that comment on and critique general assumptions and influential arguments surrounding this debate, including Irene Clark and Dave Healy's 1996 "Are Writing Centers Ethical?" and Peter Carino's 2003 "Power and Authority in Peer Tutoring." I will move on to review texts that use empirical case-study research in their arguments that CBT contexts demand a close reconsideration of the typically nondirective, hands-off approach to tutoring. Finally, foregrounding the case studies in Chapters Two-Four, I will begin to illustrate in this chapter why—precisely because the idealistic notion of "instructional flexibility" is easier said than done—arguments involving tutoring style, via the directive/nondirective continuum, offer important analytical lenses with which to scrutinize the "play of differences" that occur in various CBT situations.

"REALLY USEFUL KNOWLEDGE": THE DIRECTIVE/NONDIRECTIVE INSTRUCTIONAL CONTINUUM AND POWER AND AUTHORITY

When diving deeply into a discussion of directive/nondirective tutoring, we soon begin to realize that—as in any educational situation—we are dealing not just with methodological-instructional, but also political and personal, issues. Clark and Healy track the history of the nondirective (or noninterventionist) approach in the "orthodox writing center." They describe how in the 1970s and early 1980s, in response to open admissions, writing centers began to replace grammar drills and skills with what would become the HOCs/LOCs approach to tutoring. Along with this new instructional focus, however, came a concurrent concern—fear of plagiarism. The fear of plagiarism goes hand-in-hand with the issue of intellectual property rights—or students' rights and ownership of their own ideas and writing—a political and personal issue pertinent to tutors, students, instructors, and program directors. As we mentioned in the Introduction, this "concern with avoiding plagiarism, coupled with the second-class and frequently precarious status of writing centers within the university hierarchy, generated a set of defensive strategies aimed at warding off the suspicions of those in traditional humanities departments" like English (Clark and Healy 245; also see Nelson and Garner). For Clark and Healy, the resulting restraint on tutor method soon took on the practical and theoretical power of a moral imperative. They describe how influential essays from Evelyn Ashton-Jones, Jeff Brooks, and Thomas Thompson cemented the hands-off approach to one-to-one instruction.

Ashton-Jones juxtaposed the "Socratic dialogue" to the "directive" mode of tutoring. Drawing on Tom Hawkins, she characterized the directive tutor as "shaman, guru, or mentor," while Socratic tutors are given the more co-inquisitive label "architects and partners." Practitioners were left to wonder if it could be a good or bad thing if a tutor-tutee relationship develops to the point that the tutee looks to the tutor as somewhat of a "mentor." (And in CBT situations, especially, as we will discuss below, programs are designed with this question in mind since peer mentorship occurs on a regular basis.) Brooks, in arguing that students must take ownership of their texts, associated directive tutors with editors, good editors perhaps sometimes, but editors nonetheless. Brooks goes so far as to advise that if a tutee seems unwilling to take an active role in the tutorial, that tutors simply mimic the tutee's unengaged attitude and action. And Thompson urged tutors to avoid having a pen in hand during tutorials. In the name of the Socratic method, he also urges tutors "not to tell students what a passage means or give students a particular word to complete a thought" (Clark and Healy 246).

In an ironic twist, Clark and Healy note that "by being so careful not to infringe on other's turf—the writer's, the teacher's, the department's, the institution's—the writing center has been party to its own marginality and silencing" (254). In answer to this perceived marginality and silencing, they offer essays by Marilyn Cooper, Shamoon and Burns, and Muriel Harris, as well as the work of Lev Vygotsky, that value the pedagogical feasibility of modeling and imitation and an epistemological continuum that moves writers outside their texts to some degree. Cooper, for example, in her close reading of Brooks, argues that tutors who focus too intently on students' papers may be missing out on important chances to help students with important, more general writing issues like how the course is going in general or how to approach assignments in creative ways. For Cooper, and others, a strict minimalist approach forecloses the act of negotiation—the "really useful knowledge"—that could take place in a one-to-one, negotiation that takes both the tutor's and the tutee's goals into consideration.

Peter Carino urges writing center personnel to reconsider the importance of the too-often vilified directive tutor. Like Clark and Healy, he sets up for critique the idea of interventionist tutoring as anathema to the strict open-ended questioning style advocated by Brooks. Carino then discusses Shamoon and Burns's "A Critique of Pure Tutoring" in which the authors explain how master-apprentice relationships function in fruitful and directive ways for art and music students. In the master-apprentice relationship, the master models and the apprentice learns by imitation, from the authority of the master artist, the tricks of the trade. In that essay, Shamoon and Burns also suggest the importance of imitation to classical-rhetorical education. Reflecting on Clark and Healy's essay, Carino concurs that nondirective approaches are defense mechanisms resulting from the marginalized history of writing centers within the university and their subsequent paranoia over plagiarism. Further, Carino applauds how Nancy Grimm advocates the directive approach so that traditionally marginalized or under-prepared students are not barred from access to mainstream academic culture. (I will continue this discussion below.)

Conclusively, Carino suggests a dialectical approach to the directive/nondirective dilemma, implying that directive tutoring and hierarchical tutoring are *not* synonymous:

> In short, a nonhierarchical environment does not depend on blind commitment to nondirective tutoring methods. Instead, tutors should be taught to recognize where the power and authority lie in any given tutorial, when and to what degree they have them, when and to what degree the student has them, and when and to what degree they are absent in any given tutorial. (109)

He offers a seemingly simple equation for when to be direct and when to be nondirect: the more knowledge the student holds, the more nondirective we should be; the less knowledge the student holds, the more directive we should be. (Suggesting the roles specialist and generalist tutors might also play.) He wisely, affectively qualifies this suggestion, however, by stating that shyer but more knowledgeable students might need a combination of directive prodding to urge them to take responsibility for their work and nondirective questioning to encourage them to share their knowledge, while chattier but less knowledgeable students could benefit from nondirective questions to help curb hasty, misdirected enthusiasm, and directive warnings when they are making obviously disastrous moves. Unfortunately, Carino does not also characterize what to do when the *tutor* holds more or less subject matter or rhetorical knowledge, or when the tutor is shyer or chattier. And this is where current research in CBT can help explore this question. And this is also where the terms directive/nondirective can be compared to other closely related pedagogical concepts like control/flexibility (Gillespie and Lerner). Interestingly, Carino points to the dichotomy of power and authority that has historically existed between the classroom and the center, complementing and amplifying Clark and Healy's notion of fear of plagiarism. Because centers have a "safe house" image compared to the hierarchical, grade-crazed image of the classroom, writing center practitioners feel the need to promote a nondirective approach, which they view as sharply contrasting the directive, dominating, imposing nature of the classroom. This attitude has led to some pretty confining dictums—like tutors not holding a pen or pencil in their hand—that can unintentionally hinder helpful teaching and learning.

A minimalist philosophy may sometimes actually cause tutors to (un)intentionally withhold valuable knowledge from students. Muriel Harris recounted in 1992 how a student rated her as "not very effective" on a tutor evaluation because she was trying to be a good minimalist tutor; the student viewed her as ineffective, explaining, "she just sat there while I had to find my own answers" (379). Although we could certainly question the student's perceptions, the fact that one of writing centers' most valuable players, admittedly, might sometimes drop the ball prompts us to continue questioning the writing center's dualized directive/nondirective philosophies. Yet if we do a double-take on Harris's views on this issue, we see that she has always seen both approaches as important. Clark and Healy point to an earlier work of Harris's from *College English* in 1983 "Modeling: A Process Method of Teaching" in which Harris advances a much more directive approach. In describing the benefits of intervening substantially in students' writing processes Harris asks "what better way is there to convince students that writing is a process that requires effort, thought, time, and persistence than to go through all that writing, *scratching out, rewriting, and revising* with and for our students?" (qtd. in Clark and Healy 251; emphasis added). Harris, early on, like Shamoon and Burns, understood the value and importance of the ancient rhetorical tradition of modeling and imitation *in the service of invention and style.* In order to perform such moves as "scratching out" and "rewriting" tutors must have some confidence in their ability (the theoretical and practical feasibility and kairotic timeliness involved) in offering more directive and traditionally "risky" and potentially intrusive suggestions on issues of substance and style.

"WHAT SORT OF MESSAGE ARE WE SENDING?" TOWARD A HUMBLE/SMART BALANCE

The issues presented above—questions of tutor authority, role negotiation, and instructional method and style—while immediately relevant for CBT, also parallel important, somewhat more general, scholarship in writing center theory and practice and student-teacher writing conferences, scholarship with methodological strengths and weaknesses that reflect our field's developing understanding over time. Laurel Black's *Between Talk and Teaching* offers a rigorous examination of the assumptions teachers bring to one-to-one conferences with their students, assumptions applicable for all teachers of writing. Black opens her book with the concept of conferences as one-to-one conversations, which may or may not use the student's text as the prime mover of conversation. Black points to Lad Tobin's view of the genealogy of conferencing from "first generation" teacher-focused to "second generation" student-focused conferences in which both leave all agency in the hands of the teacher. What Tobin, and in turn Black, look to is a "third generation" of conferencing "that takes into account the dynamic relationship aspects of each writing conference: the student's relationship to the text, the teacher's relationship to the text, and the student's and teacher's relationship to each other" *through conversation* (Tobin qtd. in Black 16). But Black goes on to suggest the complexity of this ideal notion of conferencing when she writes: "Warning bells should go off as we read about conference 'conversation'" (21). Black's work on writing conferences offers a rich spectrum of both the larger rhetorical issues of power and authority in conferencing with an attention to micro linguistic features and cues. The strength of Black's work lies in the acknowledgment and exploration of the complexity of conferences as a speech genre in which, as in one-to-one tutorials, a delicate balance is sought between conversational talk and teaching talk. Black sees the complex interplay between the cognitive, social, and linguistic as contributing forces—to varying degrees, at different locations, in specific moments—to the unstable speech genre that is one-to-one conferencing (echoing to some degree our discussion of the generic "play of differences" in CBT from the Introduction). Yet in Black's analysis of conference transcripts we do not hear the students' point of view, nor the instructors', nor do we get any real sense of what the pre-conference relationship between the students and the instructors are like.

The work of Nancy Grimm, which also displays a concern for the cognitive, social, and linguistic forces in one-to-one teaching, has made a major impact on the ways writing center professionals (re)view their theory and practice. Yet, like Black, her research falls short of providing the surrounding contextual information necessary to make full use of her findings. Her conceptualization of directive/nondirective tutoring can also be held up to scrutiny. In her concise yet theoretically sophisticated 1999 *Good Intentions*, Grimm juxtaposes the implications of Brian Street's autonomous and ideological models of literacy to the work we do. Arguing that our traditional hands-off approach to one-to-one instruction is often misguided, she writes:

> Writing center tutors are supposed to use a nondirective pedagogy to help students "discover" what they want to say. These approaches protect the status quo and withhold insider knowledge, inadvertently keeping students from nonmainstream cultures on the sidelines, making them guess about what the mainstream culture expects or frustrating them into

> less productive attitudes. These approaches enact the belief that what is expected is natural behavior rather than culturally specific performance. (31)

Like Cooper five years earlier, Grimm calls for writing center practitioners to move away from a focus on the paper to the cultural and ideological work of literacy: negotiating assignment sheets to see if there might be any room for student creativity or even resistance; making students aware of multiple ways of approaching writing tasks and situations, making tacit academic understandings explicit; rethinking tired admonishments regarding what we cannot do when tutoring one-to-one. Grimm illustrates what a tough job this really is, though, in her analysis of Anne DiPardo's "'Whispers of Coming and Going': Lessons from Fannie."

While Grimm, drawing on Street and Delpit, forcefully argues for the importance of moving past our infatuation with nondirective tutoring, she may be inadvertently pointing to why it is also perhaps just as important for us to continue to value some of our nondirective strategies—suggesting the truly subtle nature of this issue. DiPardo's essay describes and analyzes the tutorial relationship between Morgan, an African-American tutor, and Fannie, a Navajo student who just passed her basic writing course and is attempting the required composition course. Both DiPardo and Grimm speculate that Morgan's repeated attempts to prod and push Fannie toward what Morgan believed was realization or progress, only pushed Fannie away from any productive insights. The tutorial transcript presented by DiPardo illustrates how Morgan dominated the conversation, often interrupting Fannie (though unfortunately we do not get micro-level analysis like how long pauses were after questions, etc.), how Morgan appropriated the conversation, attempting to move Fannie toward her idea of a normal academic essay. While this approach may ostensibly resemble the directive approach advocated by Grimm, Lisa Delpit, and others, what it leads Grimm and DiPardo to conclude is that tutors must be encouraged to practice "authentic listening": "As DiPardo's study illustrates, without authentic listening, the very programs designed to address social inequality inadvertently reproduce it, 'unresolved tensions tugged continually at the fabric of institutional good intentions' (DiPardo 1992, 126)" (Grimm 69; also see Clark "Perspectives," 46). Ironically, listening, or allowing the student to talk a little more during one-to-ones to enable them to supposedly be more in control of the tutorial discourse, is one of—perhaps the most fundamental of—nondirective strategies.

Carol Severino, drawing on Ede and Lunsford for her 1992 essay "Rhetorically Analyzing Collaborations," associates directive tutoring with hierarchical collaboration and nondirective tutoring with dialogic collaboration (recall Carino's words above). But her analysis of two conferences from two different tutors with the same student points perhaps more emphatically toward our assumptions of what the ideal tutoring session is *supposed* to sound like. The student is Joe, an older African American returning student taking a class entitled "Race and Ethnicity in Our Families and Lives." Severino analyzes the transcripts of sessions between Joe and Henry, a high school teacher in his thirties working on his MA in English, and Joe and Eddy, a younger freshman with less teaching experience. Like the sessions that DiPardo and Grimm analyze above, Henry uses his teacherly authority, from the very start of the conference, by asking closed or leading questions that control the flow of the rest of the tutorial. In contrast, during the session between Joe and Eddy, Eddy starts off right away asking Joe open-ended questions like how he feels about the paper, and where he wants to go from there. For Severino, this sets a more conversational, peer-like tone that carries through the rest of the tutorial. Although obviously privileging the nondirective/dialogic approach, Severino concludes by asserting that it is difficult to say which of the above sessions was necessarily "better." The problem with Severino's analysis, however, is that we do not get a clear enough picture of exactly what was going on during the tutorial. As with Fannie above, we do not know how Joe felt about the interaction. Perhaps he found greater value in Henry's more directive approach. Further, we do not know what stage of the draft Joe is in in either tutorial (information that might have contributed to the level of directive or nondirective instruction). Nonetheless, the value in Severino's overall argument involves her urging those who prepare tutors to avoid prescriptive tutoring dictums that do not take into consideration varying assignment tasks, rhetorical situations, and student personalities and goals—the "always" and "don't" that can close off avenues for authentic listening and conversation.

Four, more recent, case studies, while also having their limits, inch us closer toward building feasible theoretical frames and methods for analyzing the deployment of—and pedagogical implications of— directive/nondirective instructional strategies. Susan Murphy's 2006 study of tutorials uses Goffman's theory of self-presentation and Brown and Levinson's theory of politeness to frame her argument that analyzing discourse strategies of self-presentation can provide clues to how tutors enact nondirective strategies. Her discourse analysis of four tutorials illustrates various graduate student tutors alternately imposing and displacing authority. One graduate tutor, working with a student on a novel the tutor is unfamiliar with, attempts to perhaps "save face" by aligning himself with the field of English, in the process using jargon like "flashback," "rhetoric," and "foreshadowing," and even going so far as to urge the student to "Go read some criticism. Develop some ideas about the book" (75, 77). On the other hand, another graduate tutor, while also displaying an alignment with the field through the use of the pronoun "we," alternately distances herself from literary critic experts and aligns herself more closely with the student writer with the pronoun "they." Murphy argues this sort of desire to save both her own face and the face of the student writer "seems to be a result of a desire to both claim and reject the authority that comes with her role as graduate student, teacher, and consultant," requiring being smart and humble simultaneously (78). In their 2012 study of tutorials, Jamie White-Farnham, Jeremiah Dyehouse, and Bryna Finer report similar issues with authority and trust in their attempts to map "facilitative" and "directive" tutoring strategies. The authors note the directive strategy of using tag questions like "right?" at the end of sentences to keep students "on board" as well as, like in Murphy's study, alignment with the authority of the instructor and the field with a phrase like "often, when teachers say that, they do mean ... " (5). Yet the authors also report having trouble definitively mapping what they call facilitative tutoring.

Two 2009 articles by Isabel Thompson and colleagues provide both breadth and depth of analyses that might help further differentiate and qualify between more directive and nondirective tutoring strategies. Thompson et al.'s "Examining Our Lore" offers a study of 4,078 conference surveys from Auburn University's English Center to ascertain how "various conference attributes related to writing center mandates affected tutors' and students' conference satisfaction" (87-88). 26 of the tutors were graduate students, and 16 undergraduates; 3,330 conferences were conducted with students enrolled in freshman composition courses. The researchers' cogent findings—based on compelling statistical data—support Carino's and others' assertions from above regarding the complex nature of traversing the directive/nondirective continuum. Students reported high satisfaction with tutorials when they felt the tutors were answering their questions; students also reported satisfaction when they felt comfortable during the conference. Despite the fact that tutors were trained in nondirective approaches, tutors reported that the more directive they were, the more satisfied they were with the conference. How much tutors talked (or conversationally "dominated" the session) or how closely tutors acted like "peers" had little statistical effect on student satisfaction. Thompson et al. ultimately support arguments from Clark ("Perspectives") that, in practice, tutors are unable to avoid being directive, and students, in fact, appreciate this directiveness. Yet, the authors are careful to qualify this claim when they assert:

> Neither our survey nor other empirical research about writing center conferences suggests totally discarding nondirective tutoring strategies. Students' efforts, feelings of being challenged, willingness to take risks, and independence are vital

> for their engagement ... tutoring strategies have been found most satisfactory when they are flexibly used—when they vary between assuring students' comfort and ownership of their writing and answering students' questions to improve writing quality. (96)

This concern with balancing tutorial methods to include attention to both acts of trying to coach students toward strategies to improve their papers (or writing in general) and the pedagogically affective is given a more focused look by Thompson in another 2009 article.

Thompson's highly detailed microanalyses of one successful tutorial session, "Scaffolding in the Writing Center," uses the frame of scaffolding to investigate how analysis of both verbal and nonverbal cues might help further contextualize directive and nondirective (or facilitative) tutoring strategies. Thompson's analyses complements and enriches Severino's discussed above, by illustrating how a peer undergraduate tutor starts off a session using more typically recognized nondirective strategies, like Eddy, to get the student writer involved and taking ownership of the paper. (Thompson characterizes the tutor and student writer as follows: "The tutor is an experienced and well-respected undergraduate male, a senior majoring in psychology, the student is a female freshman" [425].) But she also details how, as the session progresses, the tutor feels freer to deploy, like Henry, more directive strategies. What results is a more balanced humble/smart session, like the one reported by Murphy above, that both the tutor and tutee rated "highly successful." Especially promising in regards to mapping/categorizing directive and nondirective strategies is Thompson's frame of scaffolding. She divides this frame into three categories: one, direct instruction, and two that—for the sake of analysis—we might consider more facilitative or nondirective, cognitive scaffolding and motivational scaffolding. Thompson details why developing trust and comfort requires an active session where verbal cues like backchannels, pauses, and overlaps hint at the "subtle persuasion" involved in moving closer to the fruitful intersubjectivity of the coveted successful tutorial. While the directive instruction category is obviously more in line with directive strategies—giving explanations, answers or examples, or posing leading questions—and cognitive scaffolding sounds very much like nondirective strategies—demonstrating, giving part of an answer or asking an open-ended question then "fading out"—I would argue that the third category, motivational scaffolding—using humor, providing positive or negative feedback, evincing sympathy and empathy—could be considered a nuanced form of nondirective tutoring, perhaps one requiring the sort of facilitative "authentic listening" called for by DiPardo and Grimm. Visually, we might imagine directive/nondirective

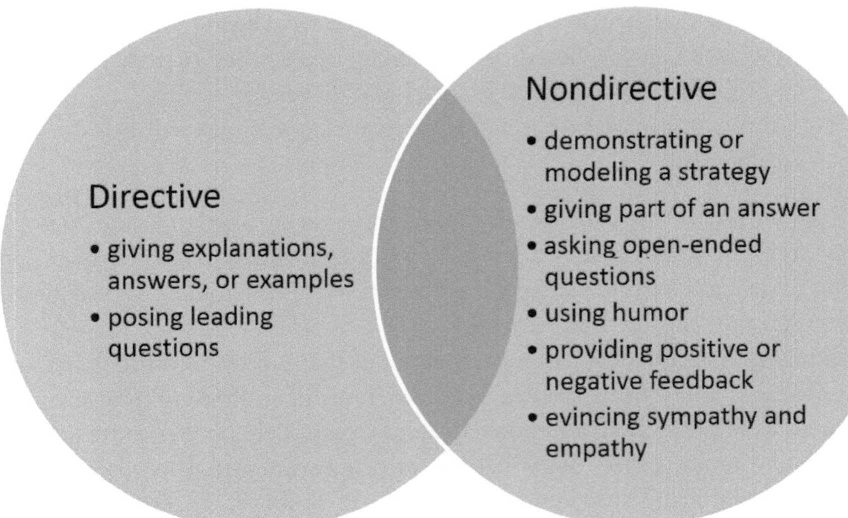

Figure 2: Overlapping reality of directive/nondirective strategies.

strategies overlapping at any given moment during tutorials, as in Figure 2.

Applying these methodological insights to CBT settings, I want to pose the same "higher risk/higher yield" question that Boquet asks in *Noise from the Writing Center* of any tutor: "How might I encourage this tutor to operate on the edge of his or her expertise?" (81). Then I want to analyze what happens when tutors must negotiate this challenging new role. What happens when a less-experienced or less-"trained" or perhaps even over-trained tutor attempts to work with a student writer? What happens when tutors—with varying levels of experience or training, with different personalities, with different notions of how they are "supposed" to act—are connected much more closely with the students and instructor of the course?

"THEY LIKE TO BE TOLD WHAT TO DO": NEGOTIATING DIRECTIVE/NONDIRECTIVE TUTORING ASSUMPTIONS WHEN MOVING BETWEEN THE WRITING CENTER AND THE DEVELOPMENTAL WRITING CLASSROOM

Above we discussed how tricky it can be to balance directive/nondirective instructional methods when teaching one-to-one. Others who have reported on their experiences as small-group peer response facilitators (often done in writing classrooms rather than at the center) have echoed these and other concerns—while also expounding on the benefits of small-group tutoring, including opening avenues for closer writing classroom/center connections and teaching students how to better tutor (peer review) each other's work (Spilman; Lawfer; Shaperenko; Corbett "Bringing," "Role"; Decker "Diplomatic"). In my earlier work on CBT, I reflect on my experiences visiting classrooms in the late 1990s and early 2000s. In the brief 2002 "The Role of the Emissary" I narrate two visits to classrooms, one where I simply discuss the services of the writing center, and the other where I actually sit in on a peer review and response session. My argument in that early essay calls for writing center tutors to boldly travel into classrooms with full confidence in their abilities to share what they've learned about learning to write. But the thinly-veiled attitude I dance in that essay was motivated by a belief touched on in the Introduction of this book: the scapegoating attitude that writing center and one-to-one tutoring is a better teaching-learning paradigm than classroom instruction. In the *On Location* chapter "Bringing the Noise," I narrate idealistic scenes involving students, tutors, and instructors getting along famously in the classroom—while illustrating how tutors can embrace more directive instructional roles that can complement more nondirective strategies during peer response facilitation (also see Decker "Diplomatic"; Anderson and Murphy; Gilewicz). I also describe how something as simple as having a tutor visit to talk about her personal experiences with academic writing can offer interpersonal points of identification and connection between tutors and students, students and the academy, and the writing center and the classroom. These sorts of experiences in traversing into classrooms, into the turf of a classroom instructor to listen to fellow students and to talk with them about whatever concerned them most at that time, would provide the impetus for further practice and future experiences. But others in the same collection offer a more conflicting view of what can occur when making the leap between center and classroom—especially when tutors trained in nondirective instructional approaches bring this more hands-off philosophy to the developmental writing classroom.

Barbara Liu and Holly Mandes, though also celebrating overall success in CBT initiatives, describe how certain adjustments had to be made to the typical nondirective approach when tutors were moved into the classroom. The authors explain the transition of moving tutors from the writing center into the classroom for their developmental writing course, English 100Plus at Eastern Connecticut State University in terms of three problematic assumptions: writers usually come to the center of their own accord; the typical one-to-one tutorial is supposed to focus on the writer not the paper; and the writing tutor's role is of learner, listener, and questioning conversation partner, not expert teacher. Liu and Mandes would soon come to realize that "the nonintrusive, writing center(ed) model in which Eastern's tutors had been trained did not always meet the needs of the students with whom they were working in the classrooms" (88).

Yet the authors maintain that less-prepared writers are often more apprehensive than mainstream student writers because they are aware of being, or have at least been identified by others as, somehow remedial. When tutors are circulating in the classroom, in their zeal to help, they can all too easily "invade the writer's comfort zone" treading "a thin line between help and invasion" (91). In building a relationship based on *trust,* tutors come to learn that the demands of on-location tutoring and mentoring may cause them to have to reevaluate and redeploy some of the most cherished pedagogical strategies learned during their tutor training.

Like Liu and Mandes, Melissa Nicolas also points to the fact that this arrangement requires students to meet with tutors, rather than the typically optional writing center meeting. In her "Cautionary Tale" we see the difficulty in tutors moving from a more writing center-like setting to an instructional setting that demands that they move beyond the role of the emissary to closer communicative contact and negotiation with teachers and students in the classroom. This new arrangement puts tutors in a high-risk situation where they may be struggling to apply what they have been taught from orthodox writing center theory and practice to this new and different instructional context. Nicolas reports how this caused authority and role confusion in the tutors. One tutor explained how, even though she tried to downplay her authority while working with students, still "they just always seem to look at me or toward me ... They like to be told what to do ... It's kind of confusing. It's sort of like a balancing act where you try not to be in it too much but try to be there, but it's like you're not there. It's hard" (120). The hard fact is that when tutors are in the classroom in the capacity of a helper or assistant of some sort it will look to students as if they must be there for a reason—the reason of course to share some knowledge or skill that the students may not necessarily possess. And just as classroom teachers either learn to balance levels of control and directiveness, questioning and listening, or just letting students run with ideas, tutors and students develop a heightened sense of these instructional moves. Here, again the idea that *student desire* for what they see as what they need, and the willingness either to oblige the student or not—or *tutor desire* to live up to the theoretical ideal tutor—is not always an easy choice for peer tutors to make. It is the double-bind that underscores each move the tutor makes whether tutoring one-to-one or collaborating in the classroom.

Finally, we must also factor into the equation that so many developmental classrooms are filled with diverse students, and diverse tutors. In relation to my treatment of Grimm DiPardo, and Severino above, Lisa Delpit insists that "there are codes or rules for participating in power; that is, there is a 'culture of power'" ("Silenced" 568) that students and teachers must negotiate. Delpit believes that those who hold power are often least aware of it, while those without it are fully aware of their marginal subject positions. Delpit further claims that explicit, direct teaching of these codes or rules enable those outside the margins of power to gain access to the resources needed for positions of power (569). Drawing on a study of cross-cultural interactions by John Gumpertz, Delpit suggests that efforts toward nondirective, power-displacing instruction may actually be less helpful for some students than more direct, power-acknowledging methods. Others (Mann; Neff; Corbett "Learning") claim that students with various learning disabilities (LDs) require tutors who are willing to take a more active, interventionist role in these students' learning to write and writing-to-learn performances. These questions of the connections between instructional method and tutor, student, and even instructor identity will resurface repeatedly in the following chapters.

RENEGOTIATING OUR BEST INTENTIONS

This review of the directive/nondirective literature begins to illustrate why scholars in writing center and peer tutoring theory and practice urge practitioners to keep our pedagogy flexible and attuned to the protean nature of peer collaborative interaction. In short, tutors need to be aware of the rhetorical complexity that any given tutorial or any given visit to a classroom can entail. This complexity means that tutor coaches should stay wary of the all-too-tempting rules of thumb and "familiar memes" Geller et al. caution against in the opening quotes that can lead to Black's "reductive binaries," unintentionally cementing strained social relationships between tutors, tutees, and instructors. Writing center and peer tutoring people are proud of our history of caring and focusing attention on the individual learner. But in our quest to always be the good guys, the guide on the side rather than the sage on the page, have we alienated some outside our centered family circles? Harking back to the parent genres in the Introduction, in dramatistic terms, Burke writes that the scapegoat is "in effect a kind of 'bad parent,'" and that "the alienating of inequities from the self to the scapegoat amounts to a *rebirth* of the self. In brief, it would promise a conversion to a new principle of motivation—and when such a transformation is conceived in terms of the familial and the substantial, it amounts to a change of parentage" (*Grammar* 407). Writing center practitioners—like many writing teachers—have perhaps played the blame game too often and for too long, resulting in lopsided theory and practice. Whether blaming the classroom/center discursive goat—plagiarism, teacher assignments, grades—or the directive/nondirective instructional goat, writing center scholarship grapples with ways practitioners might continue to reevaluate and revise our best intentions. CBT theory and practice seeks to reclaim the consubstantiality of the writing center and the writing classroom: moving the idea of a writing center dramatically from physical place to theoretical and practical space, enlarging and enriching the scope of teaching one-to-one and in small groups, and creating a larger arena for rhetorical investigation, reconsideration, and reevaluation.

We can reevaluate the importance of the classical-rhetorical idea of modeling and imitation in the service of invention, arrangement, style, and delivery—in short, in learning how to learn and teach writing. Adding the idea of modeling, a willingness to sometimes take a more hands-on approach to tutoring, can complement a tutor's instructional repertoire. Tutor coaches (be they directors, or more experienced co-workers) can offer suggestions—or models, or examples—of when it might be more or less appropriate to be more or less directive or nondirective. Something as fundamental as asking a student at the beginning of a tutorial what phase their draft is in, a question that neither Healy and Clark nor Carino address, could go a long way toward setting up just how hands on or off a tutor can be (or how much researchers can surmise from tutorial transcripts). We can (and often do) realize that sometimes it's all right to give a pointed suggestion, to offer an idea for a subtopic, to give explicit direction on how to cite MLA or APA sources, (in later drafts) to offer examples of alternate wording and sentence constructions, in short, to practice along a continuum of instructional choices both collaborative *and* empowering, allowing for alternate moments of interpersonal and methodological collegiality *and* agency-building. Once we feel that our best intentions more closely match our potential for best practices, we can find ways to further question and more rigorously examine these reconsidered notions.

But how well will all my effusive rhetoric above regarding directive and nondirective tutoring—"tutoring on the edge of expertise," cultivating instructional "flexibility" or a "smart/humble" balance—hold up under both macro-contextual and micro-analytical scrutiny? In the remaining chapters I will undertake one of the most rigorous examinations of in-the-field practices of tutors, instructors, students, and coordinator engaging in the close collaboration of CBT ever attempted. The same questions concerning directive/nondirective tutoring philosophy and strategy and CBT we've been touching on in this chapter will resurface, but in much greater depth and detail: How do tutors in various CBT scenarios deal with walking the fine line between collaboration and plagiarism, between intervention and invasion? How does more intimate knowledge of course content, teacher expectations, and/or closer interpersonal connections between teachers and students, affect the ways tutors deploy directive and nondirective strategies? How does tutor training in directive/nondirective strategies and philosophies hinder or enhance their interactions with student writers? And returning to that central question from the introduction: How can what we know about peer tutoring one-to-one and in small groups—especially the implications of directive and nondirective tutoring strategies and methods brought to light in my and others' case studies—inform our work with students in writing centers and other tutoring programs?

The above scenarios reported in the literature begin to clearly illustrate just how complicated things can get when you combine various instructional aspects of the parent genres, as well as different participant personalities, goals, and instructional experiences and backgrounds. These scenarios take us closer to an understanding of how authority, trust and directive/nondirective method negotiation intertwine to either deter or promote successful CBT partnerships. But in the next chapter I will begin to offer readers a set of methods and methodological tools that will enable a much deeper multi-perspectival, triangulated view of how these pedagogical issues played out in my case-study research. While scholars caution practitioners and experimenters that tutors may need to be more or less directive when interacting more closely with instructors and courses, my study suggests just how tricky this notion really is. I'll report on tutors whose performances shattered my expectations: tutors with much experience who talked too much and listened too little; conversely, tutors who held back so much that students felt like these tutors weren't doing all they could to help, or tutors with very little experience identifying—and making meaningful connections—with teachers and fellow students.

CHAPTER TWO

METHODS AND METHODOLOGY: LOCATING PLACES, PEOPLE, AND ANALYTICAL FRAMES

> If talk, conversation, and teaching are at the center of a writing center's praxis and pedagogy, then it only makes sense that we should continue using every technique in our methodological tool kit to study and understand them.
>
> – Michael Pemberton

> For a classroom-based tutoring program to succeed in providing a multivoiced forum for discussion of student writing, the assessment of that program itself needs to be multivoiced.
>
> – Jane Cogie, Dawn Janke, Teresa Joy Kramer, and Chad Simpson

My current work in CBT follows Burke's methodological imperative in an attempt to "use all that there is to use" (*Philosophy* 23) in case study research of CBT. The research methods employed are designed to be multi-method (Liggett, Jordan, and Price; Corbett "Using") and RAD or replicable, aggregate, and data-supported (Haswell; Driscoll and Perdue). Thompson et al. arguably hint at a difference between the typical writing center tutorial and the types of teaching and learning that can occur in CBT when they claim, "It is likely that students come to writing centers to improve the grades on their essays and that they expect to feel comfortable during conferences, However, they do not come to writing centers to form peer relationships with tutors" (96). As we've touched upon in this book, one of the more potentially positive occurrences afforded by the closer classroom/center interaction is the tighter interpersonal relationships that can form among the participants, including student writers and tutors. Yet this closer connection is precisely why our methods and methodology must be more nuanced. As the rhetorical situations for participants become more seemingly over-determined, our tools of analyses must become even more fine-grained and triangulated to pinpoint and make transparent any possibly determinable variables.

An important action this multi-method triangulation allows is the ability to identify rhetorical and linguistic patterns between one-to-one tutorials and peer response group facilitation. As mentioned in relation to peer response groups in the Introduction, Thompson et al. posit that, in order to get a closer understanding of the way dialogic collaboration is reciprocally realized across tutorial practices, it would be edifying to compare the discourse features of one-to-one tutoring with peer response sessions. This is an especially important consideration for CBT and the complicating play of differences that occur as peer tutors attempt to facilitate peer response groups in the classroom. In the following sections (and again in Chapter Four), I begin my attempt to address what Thompson et al. call for in terms of the comparative analyses of the discourse of one-to-one tutorials and peer response facilitation we started reviewing in the previous chapters.

DATA COLLECTION INSTRUMENTS

In order to get multiple points of view from the case study participants Table 2-1 explains the data collection instruments employed as well as why these particular tools were used.

In the following sections, I describe the settings the participants were recruited from and operated in, and introduce the participants for each respective team. I also spend some time explaining in greater depth my methods and methodologies for analyzing tutorial transcripts and peer response groups for the sessions detailed in Chapters Three and Four. In this extended methodological frame, I outline some of the strengths and weaknesses of other studies of tutorial transcripts and explain steps I've taken to account for these strengths and weaknesses in my own methods and methodologies.

SETTINGS

In order to start building a clear-as-possible picture of the context surrounding the four UW and two SCSU teams involved at the time these case studies were conducted, I will explain the two UW writing center settings that the tutors hailed from and worked at, as well as the context of how the SCSU tutors were recruited.

The first, the English Department Writing Center (EWC), I am quite familiar with, having worked there as an assistant director from 2000-2008. During the time these case studies were conducted, the EWC offered a tutor training course in writing center theory and practice unique at the UW campus, English 474. In this five-credit course tutors are introduced to the fundamentals of one-to-one instruction. They read from a course packet that includes over

Table 2-1. Data collection instruments

Instruments	Purpose and Function
End-of-term interviews with all writing instructors (graduate TAs) and tutors	Intended to ascertain the background experiences of tutors and TAs, to get an overall sense of their perceptions of how their interactions went, to get an idea of what they perceived as their roles, and to see what suggestions or recommendations they might have for better practice. Designed also to get a sense from TAs and tutors how they felt the other participants in their groups, including students, reacted and how this interaction compared to their previous experiences with tutors or tutoring (see Appendix A for interview questions).
Hand-written field notes of in-class peer response sessions	Collect and identify data for both micro-level linguistic analyses and analyses of broader rhetorical frameworks in small-group peer response sessions, and to allow for comparative analyses to one-to-one tutorials (see Categories and Codes for Analyzing Tutorial Transcripts and Small-Group Peer Response Sessions, and Figure 4, below).
End-of-term student questionnaires (see Appendix B)	Designed to get an overall idea of how students felt about their in-class and one-to-one interactions with their tutors, and to gather students' comparative impressions of this experience in relation to other tutoring experiences they've had.
End-of-term student course evaluations	Intended to gather a sense of what students thought about the course and instructor (and tutor) as a whole.
Tutor notes and journals	Intended to supplement and enrich interview and field note data, to ascertain more personalistic observations and reflections.
Course materials, including assignments and syllabi	Intended to provide context for analyses of one-to-one audio recordings, field observations, interviews, and tutor notes/journals
Audio-recordings of 36 one-to-one tutoring sessions (from the UW teams)	Intended to gather data to micro-analyze linguistic features and cues of one-to-one tutorials, in relation to broader rhetorical frameworks. Also intended to collect contextual and linguistic data that can be used to comparatively analyze small-group peer response sessions (see Categories and Codes for Analyzing Tutorial Transcripts and Small-Group Peer Response Sessions, and Figure 4, below).

twenty-two influential essays and book excerpts; they write argumentative essays on related topics; and they interact in a collaborative classroom environment that revolves around class discussion of readings and peer response workshops of each other's writing. Tutors are required to observe two one-to-one sessions from experienced fellow tutors before they begin tutoring themselves. Sessions are allotted up to fifty minutes. Once they arrive in the Center to begin practicing what they've been studying, tutors find themselves surrounded, easily within listening distance, of other new and experienced tutors conducting tutorials. Often tutors begin to talk informally about everything under the sun between sessions (see Decker, "Academic (Un)Seriousness"). While tutors read essays that describe both directive and nondirective approaches (for example Brooks; Clark, "Collaboration") the "Mission Statement" for the Center, at the time of this study posted conspicuously on the wall at the Center for all to read, leaned much more toward the minimalist approach. Figure 3 details what tutors "will and will not" do, a chart excerpted directly from the end of the statement. From my experience, the EWC served primarily mainstream students, many from the UW's mainstream FYC course English 131. All of the tutors I had worked with in CBT initiatives in the past had come from the EWC, including three of the tutors in this study: Megan, Sam, and Julian. Though I had experimented widely with having tutors attached directly to my composition classrooms on a regular basis, the majority of our CBT efforts involved sending tutors into classrooms for briefer peer review and response facilitations (Corbett, "Bringing," "The Role"; Corbett and Guerra; Corbett and LaFrance; Decker "Diplomatic"; Cogie et al.).

The second UW setting, the Instructional Center (IC), a division of the Office of Minority Affairs, provides tutorial services for a variety of courses and subjects (including a writing center) designed for "at risk" students at the UW. I first came into contact with the IC writing center while teaching for the Educational Opportunity Program (EOP), a program that coordinates classes like

Tutors will collaborate in ...	**Tutors will not ...**
Brainstorming, outlining, and discovering pre-writing strategies	Generate ideas
Developing and clarifying thesis statements	Suggest or reword thesis
Developing organizational strategies	Suggest an organization
Recognizing where elaboration or clearer transitions are needed	Provide vocabulary
Determining how and when to document outside sources	Analyze reading materials
Recognizing when more research is needed to support claims	Supply content

Figure 3: English Department Writing Center Mission Statement excerpt

the two-quarter stretch FYC course, English 104/105, jointly with the Expository Writing Program (EWP). During a visit to the IC in 2003 I spoke with representatives there about the CBT initiatives we had been working on at the EWC. This piqued their interest, and began a relationship that included IC tutors visiting my EOP classrooms to help with peer response. I approached IC administrators again for this study and they found a tutor, Madeleine, willing to participate. I also volunteered as a peer tutor for the IC writing center Spring quarter 2007. During this experience I saw the professional tutors that work for the IC working side-by-side with undergraduate, a couple of graduate, and a couple of volunteer tutors. Interestingly, at the time of this study, the IC did not provide new tutors formal training in writing center theory and practice. New tutors were offered the option of observing sessions with more experienced tutors, if they so desired. In contrast to the EWC, there is no real time limit to sessions, so one-to-ones can easily go over an hour; students can work on their writing and work with tutors intermittently. Like the EWC, the space at the IC is rather small; tutorial sessions are conducted well within hearing distance of each other. So instead of receiving structured and systematic training, new tutors learn on-the-job, through trial and error, and by listening, observing, and talking with experienced tutors. Finally, in contrast to the conspicuously-posted "Mission Statement" of the EWC, the IC has no such mission statement for their writing center. Rather than have methodological mandates, writing tutors for the IC learn very much by trial and error.

The participants from the third setting at SCSU, in contrast to the UW tutors, did not originate from a writing center. When I took the job as co-coordinator of the Composition Program at SCSU, New Haven, in the fall of 2008, I was immediately confronted with more of the same sort of developmental learners I had worked with at the UW: students with lower SAT scores, first-generation and working-class students, more students with learning disabilities—in short, students who needed and could benefit from more focused individualized instructional support. Fresh from my CBT experiences and studies at the UW, I wanted to follow up on what I believed were some of the more successful components of those studies. I felt that something unique and full of potential took place, especially with Madeleine's Team Three detailed below. So I asked Mya, one of our top instructors of our basic writing course English 110, if she would be interested in participating in this study, and if she had a tutor in her current course she might recommend as a course-based tutor for her subsequent course. She asked the student she had in mind, Gina, and Gina agreed. What followed were two back-to-back terms that illustrate what can happen when continuity between participants in CBT occurs. None of the SCSU teams received any special training to prepare them for their roles as course-based tutors. Rather, they all originated from Mya's 110 courses, a course that emphasized writing process pedagogies like multiple drafts and peer review and response sessions.

I have lingered on this discussion of settings in order to emphasize the importance of the preparatory environment (preexisting context) that underscores the one-to-one and classroom-based tutoring that occurred in the UW and SCSU case studies. I will touch on possible implications of the differences in these settings' instructional practices and (where applicable) philosophies in later sections.

PARTICIPANTS

In this section I will introduce the six teams involved in the case studies, the first four from the UW, and the fifth and sixth from SCSU. Readers will begin to get to know the participants and the respective CBT models they worked together in. Later, in Chapters Three and Four where applicable, participants will detail their impressions of how their interactions with students and with each other played out in one-to-one tutorials and classroom peer response sessions and other in-class collaborations. The two models employed were the **in-class** model and the **writing advisor** model. Essentially, the in-class model had tutors embedded in the classroom on a day-to-day basis, while the writing advisor model involved tutors much less in the classroom. Details for each TA/tutor team, respectively, are provided below.

Team One: Julian and Anne

Julian, from **Team One**, is a white, senior English/Comparative Literature major who had worked in the EWC for two years, including a quarter as an in-class tutor with me. Julian commented minimally on papers and met one-to-one with students at the EWC. He also attended two in-class peer reviews. He has the most experience tutoring one-to-one and in the classroom of all the tutors. Having worked with Julian very closely for two years prior to this study, I found him outspoken and highly intelligent.

Anne is a white, third year TA in English Language and Rhetoric. She had one year of teaching experience with first-years prior to this pairing. She had extensive training and experience, about five years, teaching one-to-one for the EWC and CLUE (CLUE, or the Center for Learning and Undergraduate Enrichment, is another campus student-support service that houses an evening writing center.) She had also presented at several national and regional writing center and Composition and Rhetoric conferences.

Table 2-2. Team One descriptions

The Model	The Tutor	The Instructor
Writing Advisor Tutor Tutor commented on papers and met one-to-one with students at the English Department Writing Center (EWC). He attended two in-class peer response sessions.	Julian is a white, senior English/Comparative Literature major who had worked in the EWC for two years, including a prior quarter as an in-class tutor. He had the most experience tutoring one-to-one and in the classroom of all the tutors.	Anne is a white, third year TA in Language and Rhetoric. She had taught two years of traditional FYC prior to this pairing. She had extensive training and experience in tutoring one-to-one for the EWC.

Table 2-3: Team Two descriptions

The Model	The Tutor	The Instructor
In-Class Tutor Tutor attended class every day and worked one-to-one with students at the English Department Writing Center (EWC).	Megan is a white, senior Communications/ English major with two years tutoring in the EWC. She planned to pursue K-12 teaching. Like all the EWC tutors (except Sam) she took a 5-credit course in writing center theory and practice.	Laura is a second year, Chinese international grad student and TA in English Literature. She had one year of teaching experience in a traditional first-year composition (FYC) classroom prior to this pairing.

Team Two: Megan and Laura

Team Two includes Megan and Laura. Megan attended class every day and worked one-to-one with students at the EWC. Megan is a white, senior Communications/English major who had been tutoring at the EWC for two years. She was planning to pursue K-12 teaching. Like all the EWC tutors (except Sam) she took a five-credit course in writing center theory and practice. Megan considered herself not the strongest writer. During her interview she described how struggling with an English class, from which she eventually earned a 4.0, persuaded her to apply to the EWC. Having worked with her an entire summer, to me Megan always seemed very nice (often "bubbly") and approachable.

Laura is a second year TA and Chinese International student, focusing on postcolonial studies and Asian-American literature. She had one year of teaching experience with first-years prior to this pairing.

Team Three: Madeleine and Sydney

Due to her schedule, Madeleine, from **Team Three**, attended class every other day and worked one-to-one with students at the IC. Madeleine is an African-American sophomore English (creative writing) major who had worked for the IC only one quarter prior to this pairing. She enjoys performing spoken-word poetry. She did not receive any formal training in one-to-one teaching prior to this pairing. She attended a college prep high school and participated in running start. Prior to this study, I was not familiar with the personality or tutoring patterns of Madeleine.

Sydney, a woman of color (African-American) herself, is a second year TA studying nineteenth- and twentieth-century African-American literature. She had about five years of teaching and tutoring experience with high school students and one year of teaching with first-years prior to this pairing. On her wish-list, Sydney had written me a note asking, if at all possible, for a tutor of color. Serendipity worked in her favor in the form of Madeleine, whom I would later learn was the only IC tutor willing to participate in this study.

Table 2-4: Team Three descriptions

The Model	The Tutor	The Instructor
In-Class Tutor Tutor attended class every other day and worked one-to-one with students at her Center.	Madeleine is an African-American, sophomore creative writing major who had tutored one quarter for her Center prior to this pairing. She did not receive any formal training in teaching one-to-one.	Sydney is a second year, African-American TA in English Literature. She had several years of teaching experience with high school students and one year teaching traditional FYC prior to this pairing.

Table 2-5: Team Four descriptions

The Model	The Tutor	The Instructor
Writing Advisor Tutor Tutor commented on student papers and met one-to-one with students at her Center. She visited class only once to introduce herself.	Samantha (Sam) is a white, senior English/Biology major who had worked in her Center for a total of two years. She had read several articles on writing center theory and practice prior to tutoring.	Sarah is a second year, Latina TA in English Literature. She had one year of teaching experience in a traditional FYC classroom prior to this pairing, and two years of experience teaching ESL.

Team Four: Sam and Sarah

Team Four includes Samantha (Sam) and Sarah. Sam commented on student papers and met one-to-one with students at the EWC. She attended class only *once* to introduce herself. Sam is a white, senior double English/Biology major who had worked as a tutor for the EWC and for the Dance Program for a total of two years. Although she is the only EWC tutor who did not take the five-credit training course, she had read several articles on writing center theory and practice and co-authored an article on group tutoring and personal statements. When I originally interviewed Sam, she seemed very shy and reserved. I was actually slightly concerned that she might be too reserved for peer tutoring (more on this later).

Sarah is a Latina, second year TA, focusing on nineteenth-century American literature. She had one year of teaching experience with first-years prior to this pairing. She also had two years' experience tutoring ESL students.

Team Five: Gina and Mya

Gina, from **Team Five**, is a white sophomore who plans on majoring in nursing. She attended class every day, did all of the course readings, and gave comments to some student papers outside of class. She said she felt her experiences as a student in English 110 with Mya, the term just prior to this one, prepared her well for her role as a course-based tutor because Mya worked with students just as much on general skills for succeeding in college as on their writing skills. She admitted that, while previous peer response experience helped prepare her for her tutoring role, she tried harder when helping students with peer response for this course than she did as a "student" in the previous course. As readers will hear more about in Chapter Four, Gina worked closely in the class with an

Table 2-6: Team Five descriptions

The Model	The Tutor	The Instructor
In-Class Tutor Tutor attended class every day, did all of the course readings, and gave comments to some student papers outside of class.	Gina is a white sophomore who plans on majoring in Nursing. She had taken English 110 with the instructor, Mya, the previous Fall term. She had no previous experience tutoring or teaching.	Mya is a white, adjunct instructor with about ten years teaching college first-year composition, two years teaching high school, and fifteen years as a home educator prior to this case study.

autistic student, Max. Having a learning disability (LD) herself, dyslexia, she understood that Max might need a little more help and attention.

The instructor, Mya, is a white, adjunct instructor with about ten years teaching college first-year composition, two years teaching high school, and fifteen years as a home educator prior to this case study. She said she already had a "bond" with Gina, since they were together in English 110. Mya then let me know about Gina's LD. She was aware that Gina has trouble understanding and comprehending what she reads.

Team Six: Kim, Penny, and Jake

Team Six enjoyed a unique partnership wherein one instructor, Jake, was assigned an in-class tutor, Kim and Penny, for each of his two sections. As mentioned above, like Gina, both tutors had been students in Mya's 110 course the previous term. Kim is a Latina freshman who planned on majoring in nursing. She had no previous experience tutoring or teaching. Interestingly, Kim had been in the same peer response group as Max, the autistic student that Sara from Team Five above worked closely with. Penny is a white, freshman Education major. She also had no previous experience tutoring or teaching.

Jake is a white, adjunct instructor with about five years teaching college first-year composition prior to this case study, including several developmental writing courses. Jake talked about how Kim and Penny had different personalities and approaches, Kim more outgoing and vociferous and Penny more reserved. He said that he actually encouraged this diversity, "letting students [tutors] find their own way."

CATEGORIES AND CODES FOR ANALYZING TUTORIAL TRANSCRIPTS AND SMALL-GROUP PEER RESPONSE SESSIONS

As described above, the one-to-one tutorials presented in Chapter Three were audio-recorded. The data for the small-group sessions reported in Chapter Four are from my field notes. Tutors, instructors, and students were solicited for their impressions of both. And all course materials, including assignments, were collected for this study. Drawing largely on Black, Harris, Gillespie and Lerner, and Gilewicz and Thonus, rhetorical and conversation discourse analyses are the primary methods for coding and analyzing one-to-one tutorial transcripts. The analyses will offer broader rhetorical frameworks as well as ways to analyze linguistic features and cues that can also be used to analyze small-group peer response sessions. Attention to how the linguistic features of tutorial transcripts

Table 2-7: Team Six descriptions

The Model	The Tutors	The Instructor
In-Class Tutors Tutors attended class every day, and gave comments to several student papers outside of class.	Kim is a Latina freshman who plans on majoring in Nursing. She had taken English 110 with the instructor, Mya, the previous Fall term. She had no previous experience tutoring or teaching. Penny is a white, freshman Education major. She had taken English 110 with the instructor, Mya, the previous Fall term. She had no previous experience tutoring or teaching.	Jake is a white, adjunct instructor with about five years teaching college first-year composition prior to this case study, including several developmental writing courses.

hint at larger rhetorical issues complicates and enriches Grice's "tacit assumption of cooperation," outlined in his conversational maxims of quality, quantity, manner, and relevance (see Blum-Kulka 39-40), in relation to CBT. As Carolyn Walker and David Elias's frequently cited analysis of teacher-student conference transcripts argued—and, in relation to tutor-tutee conferences, Thompson et al.'s study supports—the quantity or ratio of student to teacher talk did not affect either participants' perceptions of the conference's effectiveness. What this suggests is that even though writing center practitioners talk much about the value of getting students to do most of the talking, students themselves often tacitly assume that teachers or tutors *will* do most or much of the talking, and if they do not then the students' expectations might be disrupted.

Harris's "Why Writers Need Writing Tutors" provides an overarching rhetorical framework for how tutors can help writers. Tutors can: (1) encourage student independence in collaborative talk; (2) assist students with metacognitive acquisition of strategic knowledge; (3) assist with knowledge of how to interpret, translate, and apply assignments and teacher comments; and (4) assist with affective concerns. In *Teaching One-to-One* Harris offers seminal analyses of tutorials from Roger Garrison and Donald Murray, as well as tutors (though these tutors are not categorized as peer or professional or graduate students). These transcript analyses offer a useful overview of directive and nondirective methods, ways tutors help students acquire writing strategies, techniques for active listening (including listening for student affective concerns), and how questions can be used in various ways with different effects.

Gillespie and Lerner supply further analysis from tutorials, though most of the tutorial transcripts they analyze are between undergraduate writers and graduate tutors. They extend many of Harris's findings, especially in regards to the complex way various questioning techniques and strategies affect the control and flexibility of any given tutorial. In asserting "questions aren't necessarily a nondirective form of tutoring" (112) their analyses of tutorial transcripts reveal content-clarifying questions, three types of open-ended questions (follow-up, descriptive meta-analysis, and speculative), as well as directive questions that lead tutors away from the conversation advocated for by most writing center scholars to their appropriation of one-to-one tutorials. (Although, Thompson and Mackiewicz offer an important caveat. In their study of questions used by experienced tutors in 11 one-to-one conferences the authors found that "it is not possible to describe a 'good' question outside of the context in which it occurs, and even in context, the effects of questions are difficult to determine" [61].) One of the most important suggestions the authors make involves note-taking as an important aspect of tutorials. They advise tutors to read the entire paper before offering any suggestions, taking careful notes so that students can walk away with a transcript of what happened. Otherwise, the authors explain, much of what went on during the conversation will be lost, tutors may make unnecessary comments, and tutors may be too controlling or directive during the session (also see Harris, *Teaching* 108).

But both Harris and Gillespie and Lerner, due to their goals of training often beginning tutors, fall short of pushing the analysis of transcripts to the micro-linguistic level. Black and Gilewicz and Thonus offer discourse analysis of conference and tutorial transcripts that can help link the macro-rhetorical issues to the micro-linguistic features and cues of one-to-ones. Like Harris, and Gillespie and Lerner, Black pays careful attention to the issue of directive and nondirective conferencing strategies (also drawing on Garrison and Murray). Black takes the idea of typical classroom discourse, characterized by initiation-response-evaluation, an arguably directive form of instruction (see Cazden 30-59), and shows how it makes its way, often unintentionally, into conference talk. Importantly, Black applies both conversation and critical discourse analysis to the examination of one-to-one conferences. Black also explores how interruptions, backchanneling, fillers, words like "you know," can control and coerce students, "subtly forcing another speaker into a cognitive relationship that becomes a linguistic relationship that marks and cements the social relationship" (47). Like Black, Gilewicz and Thonus pay attention to pauses, backchannels, and fillers. And like Harris and Gillespie and Lerner, they are sensitive to the way questions can be used to encourage or discourage conversation. The authors take us a step further, however, in their breakdown of fillers into backchannels, minimal responses, and tag questions, their attention to pauses, and—especially relevant to this study—their subdividing of overlaps into interruptions, joint productions, and main channel overlaps. (Joint productions occur when one speaker finishes another speaker's words or phrases. Main channel overlaps happen when speakers utter words or phrases simultaneously.) For example, the authors claim that "joint productions, more than interruptions or main channel overlaps, represent movement toward greater solidarity and collaboration" (36) rather than leave all control in the hands of the tutor.

Yet, while offering important micro-level sociolinguistic analyses, both Black and Gilewicz and Thonus also fall short by not providing enough contextual information that could help readers make better sense, *or provide more of their own interpretations,* of the authors' research findings, including why tutors or teachers may be more or less directive in a given tutorial or conference. My attempt to triangulate data, to account for Erving Goffman's "wider world of structures and positions" (193) via interviews and follow-ups, transcriptions, and student questionnaires are efforts in trying to account for larger CBT contextual factors. These factors become especially important when attempting analyses of small-group tutorials.

Several elements of the analytical frame for one-to-ones discussed above also apply to small-group peer response sessions (Figure 4). All four of Harris's categories for how tutors can help writers can be highly useful as an overarching macro-frame. The use of various sorts of questions, overlaps, fillers, and frequency and length of pauses can help in the comparative micro-analyses of one-to-ones and small-group tutoring. Especially promising, as well as slightly problematic, is Teagan Decker's idea of the "meta-tutor"—a concept that provides a conceptual and analytical bridge between one-to-one and small-group tutoring and peer response. She claims that tutors leading small-group response sessions should "become meta-tutors, encouraging students to tutor each other. In this capacity, tutors are not doing what they would be doing in a one-on-one conference in the writing center, but rather they are showing students how to do it. Their role, then, does change, but at the same time remains consistent" ("Diplomatic" 27). As Decker explains, this role is different from the ones tutors typically engage in at the center. In a one-to-one setting tutors need only share what they can about the writing process, while meta-tutoring requires a level of metacognition that enables a tutor to teach students how to do what they do—but without seeming as if the tutor is withholding important information. This coaching students how to coach each other really makes tutors have to agilely balance directive/nondirective strategies. We will see in Chapter Four how this

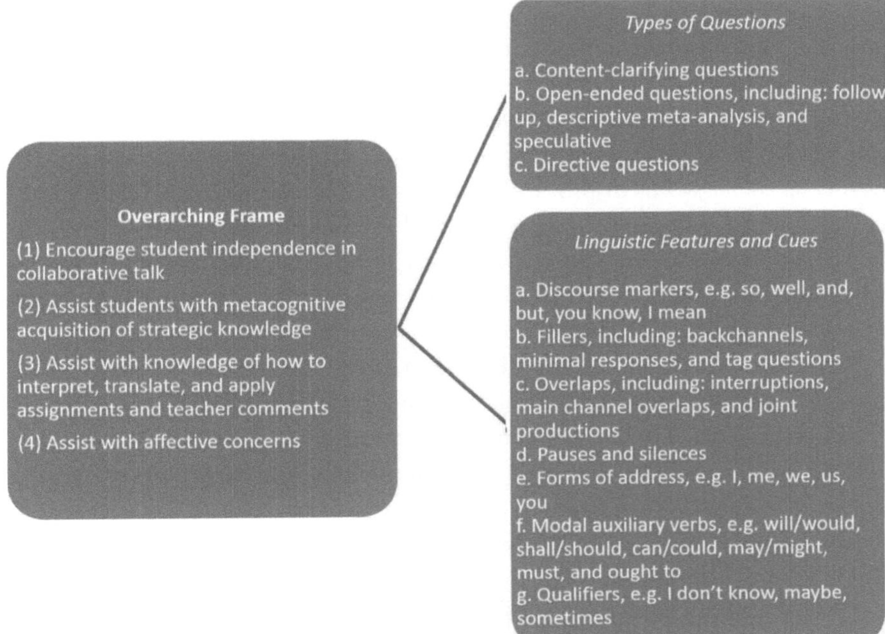

Figure 4: Macro- and micro-heuristic for coding, analyzing, and comparing one-to-one transcripts and in-class peer response field notes.

notion of the meta-tutor played out with the teams. But, first, I will turn our focus toward the balancing acts involved in the one-to-one tutorials from the UW teams.

CHAPTER THREE

MACRO- AND MICRO-ANALYSES OF ONE-TO-ONE TUTORIALS: CASE STUDIES AT THE UNIVERSITY OF WASHINGTON

> If writers are learning how to think about their writing based upon the conversations we have with them in writing center sessions, then our examination of those conversations can reveal the issues and challenges of learning to write in college and how writers learn to overcome them.
>
> – Paula Gillespie and Neal Lerner

> It's easy enough to think that once the door to that tutoring room is closed, it's only you and the writer, but the many forces swirling outside that room have not gone away.
>
> – Paula Gillespie and Neal Lerner

> What I learned from analyzing transcripts of my conferences is how great a distance lay between my image and my words, my goals and my practice.
>
> – Laurel Johnson Black

By the time I was ready to design the case studies presented in this chapter and in Chapter Four, I had already conducted several preliminary studies at the UW. For example, at the 2005 International Writing Research Conference in Santa Barbara, I presented the findings of a comparative study of tutors in Dance. I analyzed the tutorial transcripts of sessions between students in Dance and me (then a graduate student and assistant writing center director), a freshman undeclared major tutor, and a senior Dance/Russian double major tutor. The term prior to this study, the freshman tutor had apprenticed with me. I modeled for her and encouraged her to practice a more nondirective approach, centered on open-ended questions. While I likewise encouraged the Dance major tutor to use a similar approach, she did not have the benefit of a quarter's-worth of practice before the study. My findings echo Severino's from Chapter One, and Thompson and Mackiewick's study, regarding the use of open-ended questions to help students mentally work through their ideas and establish a more conversational tone to the tutorials. As with Severino's study, the freshman tutor and I had great success with Dance majors in our frequent use of nondirective, open-ended questions, while the senior Dance major was either at a loss for what to do or resorted to simply telling her peers what she thought they should do, which resulted in the tutor doing almost all of the talking during her session. This study, among others, made me very curious about the notion of "peer." It made me question just how important tutorial method really is when tutoring one-to-one. Would any tutor attempting to use a nondirective approach conduct successful tutorials? It also made me consider a related question: when, and under what circumstances, is a student ready to become a peer tutor?

In Chapter One I discussed how and why course-based tutors need, to some extent, to let go of some of the DOs and DON'Ts that can blind them to the needs of the individual student in a specific situation. But I also discussed how difficult this can be when participants are immersed in the swirl of pedagogical and interpersonal social drama involving the negotiation of the hybrid "play of differences" among and between the four parent genres. This chapter offers readers comparative micro-analyses from the 36 one-to-one tutorials conducted by the tutors from Teams One through Four. I will also compare the different accounts and points of view of participant experiences, gathered from interviews, to each other. Questions concerning directive/nondirective tutoring philosophy and strategy and CBT we discussed in the previous chapters will resurface, but in much greater depth and detail in relation to one-to-one tutorials: How does more intimate knowledge of course content, teacher expectations, and/or closer interpersonal connections between teachers and students, affect the ways tutors negotiate and deploy directive and nondirective strategies? How does tutor training in directive/nondirective strategies and philosophies hold up or play out during practice? How does negotiating the directive/nondirective continuum affect the quest for tutorly identity or reciprocal trust between participants? And what does all this have to add to our understanding of the rapport- and relationship-building that can occur in CBT, interpersonal relationships that can add value to our developing understanding of peer-to-peer teaching and learning? As I suggested in Chapter Two, it is relatively easy for researchers to pull tutorial transcripts, or field notes, or even memories out of context and interpret them in ways that best serve their rhetorical purposes. But it is another thing all together to attempt to provide enough of the preexisting contexts—as well as micro-analyses—that might allow readers to adhere more closely to my interpretations. Or better yet, to encourage readers to perhaps more readily and freely draw some of their own interpretations and conclusions as well.

Transcription notations were developed ad hoc as I coded audio-recordings. They were used for ease of voice-recognition transcription and will hopefully allow for easy reading:

> ( ) indicates interlocutor's fillers including minimal responses, backchannels, and tag questions.
>
> CAPITALIZED WORDS indicate commentary by transcriber: For example, SEVEN SECOND PAUSE indicates length of pause; INTER indicates interruption; JOINT-PROD indicates joint production (joint productions occur when one speaker finishes another speaker's words or phrases); MAINCHANOVER indicates main channel overlap (main channel overlaps happen when speakers utter words or phrases simultaneously).

AS IF SHE HADN'T SAID A WORD: JULIAN'S TUTORIALS

Julian from **Team One** had relatively little in-class interaction with the students in the course. His six tutorials all took place in the eighth week (Table 3-1). They all revolved around a major paper in which students were asked to analyze and make an argument about the rhetoric, ideology, usefulness, and feasibility of one of the topics from George W. Bush's 2006 State of the Union Address, topics including the No Child Left Behind Act; the war in Iraq; and immigration, especially the US/Mexican border. His six sessions averaged 36 minutes, with the longest lasting 53 minutes and the shortest 22 minutes. Careful analysis helps illustrate Julian's most salient tutorial pattern—the fact that he talks too much while allowing relatively much less student talk-time (or, concurrently, tutor listening-time). Couple this with the fact that he often talks a lot before he has heard the entire student's paper, and we are often left wondering why he is talking so much, often in the abstract, about the student's ideas and writing.

In session four, Julian works with a highly reticent student who is having obvious trouble negotiating the assignment. I quote this excerpt at length because it illustrates the extreme that Julian can go to in his verbosity, in his domination of the session:

> STUDENT: So right here I'm giving stats on like the casualties and stuff like that UNDECIPHERABLE
>
> JULIAN: Okay maybe try playing around actually using

Table 3-1: Linguistic features and cues from Julian's (Team One) one-to-one tutorials

Linguistic Features and Cues	Julian	Students
# of Sessions	6	
Average Length (minutes)	36	
Total Words Spoken	15,049	5,835
Average # of Words Spoken per Minute	70	27
Content-clarifying Questions	20	
Open-ended Questions	93	
Directive Questions	8	
References to TA	14	13
References to Assignment Prompt	12	1
Interruptions	28	13
Main Channel Overlaps	1	4
Joint Productions	4	9

those somehow in the opening paragraph. I'm making this up but due to to the casualties increasing the true number is blah blah blah the increased cost the cost of filling out the increased security that's where we should just maybe a framework early over to talk about what you're talking about later so they're sort of expecting it. Does that make sense (yeah) or am I just rambling? (No that makes)INTERso you guys talked about stakes a little bit right? (yeah) okay so READING STUDENT'S PAPER "although both the opposing and supporting sides make good points I would agree that we ultimately need to follow President Bush's plan and increase our troops in Iraq war." So what? I don't think you quite got the stakes there. Like literally think about it as like a bet you're making to read or write what is at stake like what are the stakes? Like in a poker game if you're writing what we did if you're wrong or like if President Bush is right and what if these things don't happen? When we lose why is this so important? I may just off-the-cuff I'm not expecting why is it important? (um)INTER I'm not expecting you to write this sentence I'm just asking you why you picked this because it's like you said it's slightly more interesting sorta grabs your attention why like what's important about what's going on here?

STUDENT: SEVERAL UNDECIPHERABLE WORDS

JULIAN: Yeah okay just get specific with it. Do you think we need to follow President Bush's plan because it affects everybody? How does it affect everybody? Like what's at stake? Like security? Like what else? What are the issues at play?

STUDENT: I don't know.

JULIAN: That's cool. Just make a note for yourself or something. I just think about it because that's the kind of stuff I read. That idea makes sense right? Just kick it around. One thing to do is if you're totally like it's not coming to you forget about it for a while because it looks like you've got a good structure of your body paragraphs right? And this last sentence suggested like talking a little about there are many clear facts like what are you talking about? See where you can end up in your conclusion like ultimately we'll only need to listen to Bush ready to do this because these things are like like why do we need to? What is President Bush saying that we need to do these things for right? So he says that we need to do this because ABC right? Do we need to do for AB and C if he's right if he's correct right? Where Bush says what we need is for AB and C and you look at that and he is right we do need to do it for these reasons one of those can be your stakes because that's what you're talking about right? You just need to introduce them in a general way. I know I'm rambling but I'm trying to say that the topics are the central ideas of your body paragraphs. You can sort of like generalize about them; just sort of go back and connect them to claim. (yeah) FIVE SECOND PAUSE That's got to actually do a lot. When I get stuck on opening paragraphs like I'll just because I don't know I don't know how the writing process goes for you but you my intro paragraph takes me and my claim takes me about as much time as writing half of my body paragraphs, so sometimes I'll write by pulling my quotes and I'll write the central paragraphs and then in writing them I'll be like oh I do have something to say in like my conclusion. I'll I'll go back and generalize to make a claim. (all right) I'm talking a lot like let me ask you a question. You guys have talked about rhetorical analysis right? So what do you think about the rhetorical analysis you have so far on Bush in this first and second paragraph?

STUDENT: I don't know what rhetorical means.

JULIAN: Okay cool. Rhetoric right the word "rhetoric" is always a like it can mean writing or speech or presentational language. I don't know who coined the term but the big famous historical thing that it comes from is like a Roman senator who taught about it TURNING TO ANOTHER TUTOR hey Kate who was the famous Roman guy who like is the famous rhetorician? Yeah yeah thank you this famous Roman guy named Cicero who was like a major slick politician. I forget what he did, but he basically swayed the populace just by like the power of his speech. So the idea is he is like not just what he says but like why do you think he said this exactly or what's he trying to accomplish with it right? So rhetoric is like using language in specific ways to accomplish specific goals. (ok)

STUDENT: The way he's saying it then he's trying to keep you're going into details and kinda like so that everybody can understand what he's talking about and because he's emotional in the words that he's, I don't know, try to explain like why Bush is basically explaining like why we need to think about sending more troops.

JULIAN: Totally, no, I think you're right on the money; like I heard you saying like he's avoiding numbers and statistics and he's using emotional language. That's awesome; that's the kind of stuff you want to get explicit and say right? But this will do more to it, so much easier to figure out you like okay I know you totally got that in, their fears. He's avoiding numbers and statistics but who is he using emotional language? Was he maybe using images that have a high impact? He talks about flying a plane at you but I heard that and I'm like I had mental images of 9/11 right? Of airplanes into the building. So you figure out what you think he's doing right? And then you've got to posit some sort of argument about why you

> think he's doing it. The first tactic I would try, because it might not be obvious at first, take a look at the issues you are talking about so if these are the issues you've identified that are applied to the Iraq war against the people are for right? Where are the issues involved with it? Monetary cost, other political things right? So how does what he says and the way he says it relate to these issues right? So like how is he positioning himself with his language upon the key issues of the debate that you've identified? That's kind of what you are being asked to do for rhetorical analysis. Does that make sense? (yes) And you've got the hard part down; you figured out the issues that you are talking about and you figured out where your key passages are. Now you got to like sort of connect them and just sort of like a sentence or two about how and why these different sentences are helping him or not helping him. Maybe you think he messed up or maybe should have said this. Bush maybe the speechwriters and you find something in stuff like that (ok). TEN SECOND PAUSE Did you talk with Anne about the feasibility, usefulness and ideological implications? (Yeah) Did that make sense? (yeah) Cool, so could you take me to your like what your thoughts are so far on this?
>
> STUDENT: Like put both the supporting and the refusal of the arguments for and some of what the opposing sides are saying some of the different ways we can go about it and how some of his things are feasible.

In this striking example, Julian, granted, is faced with an incommunicative student whose inability to grasp the assignment makes Julian's job tough. But notice how in that second interruption Julian asks a question and just as the student begins to annunciate a reply, "um," Julian jumps in with more questions. Julian's next question meets with "I don't know" which spins him on more rambling. And he knows he is rambling, which causes him to actually slow down and ask a question that leads him to figure out the student does not understand the idea of rhetorical analysis. This seems promising. Yet rather than ask some questions that might get the student thinking, allow time for a response, and maybe even write some notes, notice how Julian will ask a question, then answer it himself (ironically, almost like a "rhetorical" question). Repeatedly, as evidenced in the above passage, and continuing throughout this session, Julian asks "does that make sense?" The student invariably responds curtly with "yes," "yeah," and "I think so." Julian also uses the tag question "right?" ubiquitously. When Julian finally asks what the student's overall thoughts are, the student replies with a scanty summary of what Julian had been proselytizing about. Obviously, it's not making as much sense as the student ostensibly lets on. Examples like this appear repeatedly in Julian's tutorial transcripts. We hear repeated instances of Julian asking a question, not waiting or allowing enough pause for student response, then moving on to offer extended stretches where he tries hard to offer useful suggestions.

In his sixth tutorial, Julian's actions suggest that though he is metacognitively aware of his rather "inauthentic" listening habit, the problem is indeed a deep one. At the very beginning of the session, the student says "she [Anne] gave us this peer review thingy." As if she hadn't said a word, Julian responds: "How is your week going?" They never get back to the student's initial utterance.

Of the eight *student* questionnaires I received back, seven were primarily negative, and one positive. Several students commented that Julian did not seem to know what was going on in the course: "I thought it was going to help out but it didn't ... Didn't seem as Julian was up to date with our class assignment." Another, "he was never here in class to know what was going on." Another, "he didn't know what our class was doing (never updated)." Another, "Meeting with Julian seemed like a waste of time because he didn't really help me out or give me ideas for my papers and didn't right [sic] anything down ... Get a better in-class tutor that will actually be updated with the way our class is going and has input on our papers." Finally, evidence from the questionnaires shows that Julian was at least somewhat helpful to two students. One said that he "had good feedback on my paper." And the first student above who said "I thought it was going to help out ..." hints at what might have been if Julian had been in class more often: "He helped when he was in class but other than that, I still have to agree with it not helping at all."

PRAISE AND TEACHER'S PRESENCE: MEGAN'S TUTORIALS

Megan, from **Team Two,** ended up having 15 sessions, the most of all the tutors, including four return visits (Table 3-2). Megan was the only tutor for whom students visited more than once. Megan's sessions came in two waves: the first round included eight tutorials in the seventh week of the course, and the second included seven tutorials in the tenth or final week of the quarter (before final exams week).

The first eight tutorials dealt with short, two-page response papers on the texts from class: the movie *Wag the Dog,* and documentaries *The Living Room*

Table 3-2: Linguistic features and cues from Megan's (Team Two) one-to-one tutorials

Linguistic Features and Cues	Megan	Students
# of Sessions	8/7	
Average Length (minutes)	11/18	
Total Words Spoken	8,986/11,675	2,150/2,444
Average # of Words Spoken per Minute	102/93	24/19
Content-clarifying Questions	15/18	
Open-ended Questions	12/8	
Directive Questions	5/12	
References to TA	7/17	2/6
References to Assignment Prompt	1/1	0/0
Interruptions	8/17	26/20
Main Channel Overlaps	1/8	5/22
Joint Productions	3/8	17/23

Wars, and *From News to Entertainment*; and written texts from their course reader including excerpts from Sandra Silberstein and Michel Foucault. The sessions averaged only 11 minutes, with the shortest session lasting only six minutes and the longest lasting 31 minutes. Megan did not read the students' papers aloud, nor have them read it aloud as she normally might. She said that the sessions were so short because the papers were so short and she wanted to try to see as many students as possible. Certain patterns that pertain to subsequent sessions quickly began to surface. After clearing the way with initial questions, Megan began to fall into a clearer pattern. It seems she would begin with praise, and then lead into a critique followed quickly by a suggestion which I associate with Harris's metacognitive acquisition of strategic knowledge:

> MEGAN: Yeah (yeah), ok, cool I think you obviously have a good grasp on the readings and you could probably bring a few quotes from the reading *The Living Room Wars* in toINTER
>
> STUDENT: Oh yeah don't worry about that I've got it.
>
> MEGAN: Yeah and the movie is tricky like I said that is something that's pretty apparent to me too so I think that will be pretty easy to do. Do you have any questions or?

> STUDENT: Not really
>
> MEGAN: I know it's kinda brainstorming and you've already been thinking about it so once you kind of combine everything and start having a rough draft we can work off of that; you can come back and whatnot. It sounds like you've already thought about it and can already see the parallels and you have some good ideas. And don't be afraid, you're right it could be easier to have those two-paragraph structure, but I think that you could find a lot just using those two parts of the movie then using Bush and Clinton like that could be easily be two pages in itself. So if its two paragraphs I wouldn't worry too much about it (ok). So awesome, thanks for coming in.

Readers will immediately recognize this as the same pattern that constitutes most end-comments given on student essays. Megan starts by praising the student's "grasp on the readings" but quickly moves on to *imply* evaluation and provide suggestion. I say imply because even though Megan does not directly evaluate, she does imply evaluation by stating what is missing: direct quotes from the text. Megan follows a similar pattern in the rest of the first round of tutorials. She frequently tends to apprehensions that students voice and praises their good ideas. Yet at the same time she frequently, explicitly directs students to do what she would do, as in the case above when she advises "just using those two parts of the movie."

The seven sessions of the second round of conferences in week ten follow very similar patterns, characterized mostly by the role that the TA Laura plays, as students are negotiating the final portfolio assignment. Overlaps abound as students fully understand that their grades for the course are at stake, and that Megan may be able to help them do better on their portfolios. Students continue to voice sentence-level issue concerns and Megan continues to aid them with this, often linking these issues to larger structural and conceptual considerations. Students in this second round came to Megan hoping to hear that they were not too far off the assignment and to get suggestions for improving their papers and make the most out of the chance offered by the cover letter. In the final session in particular a student voices his concern with his grade for the course. He had visited to talk about the cover letter, and ended up easing his worry perhaps a bit through his interaction with Megan. This final session, more than any other, showed Megan's peer-like willingness to help strategize given the student's strong desire for a good grade:

MEGAN: You could kind of do it two ways. (mmhm) You could either because I don't know her as a TA like her grading at all (mm) and I don't know her from last year either (mmhm) so I have nothing MUTUAL LAUGHTER to judge her on so I would try to figure out yourself will it be better to argue can I get a 4.0 or you could also argue get an A which would be like what a 3.8 to 4.0 on it?

STUDENT: Oh okay so I should say A instead ofINTER

MEGAN: You could either way. I mean do which you think would be bestMAINCHANOVER(I feel like)do what you really want.

STUDENT: If I said I deserve a 4.0 she's going to be like ahhhh you don't really deserve a 4.0 soINTER

MEGAN: Yeah maybe like an A or something MUTUAL LAUGHTER and maybe too or you could say something like I know last time my portfolio was a 3.6 (mmhm) and I'm trying to improve on that so then at least she might be like "oh he invested himself and is trying to improve" and you have like a 3.7 to 4.0 (oh ok) which is still good. So that's something else you can say something like I'm really hoping to this revision process that by taking the class again to improve on my writing through going through the revision process again but really I'm hoping to get a better grade than I did last time on my portfolio because I got a 3.6 and I really want to improve. (ok) That would be a better way to do it. I might if it were me and you definitely (mmhm) don't have to do it like I say but this is a suggestion but I might go with (yeah) becauseMAINCHANOVER(that way I don't have to say) then she'll know that your like constantly trying to improve not only making revisions to your paper but you're also trying to improve from last timeJOINTPROD

STUDENT: Yeah and not only like I'm not asking for a grade (yeah) I'm asking for whatever she wants (yeah) to say. Okay.

MEGAN: Yeah that might be a good angle so either way-

> MAINCHANOVER(that might be a good angle I like that) whatever one you think is that yeah so either way whatever you think would be best but that might be a good way because then she'll really know like you're constantly (yeah) like even from last year you're trying to improve your grades (ok) and your revision process. (ok) Yeah I think that sounds good.

This 14 minute session was characterized by five instances of mutual laughter, 12 overlaps, and numerous fillers. Clearly this student saw the potential value of, and took an active conversational role with, Megan in helping him to negotiate the portfolio and in his rhetorical choices for presenting his case for an A in the course to Laura.

Of the nine completed *student* questionnaires I received, five were clearly positive in terms of the one-to-one tutorials: one student said the tutorial was "helpful." Another said, "Seeing her one-to-one was a lot better. I felt more comfortable." Another, "helpful because the teacher may have problems; [the tutor] acts as a mediator." Another, "It was nice to have someone to talk with about your paper one-to-one." And another that it was "more helpful" than her in-class interaction.

DIRECTING TALK AND TEXTS: MADELEINE'S SESSIONS

Madeleine, from **Team Three**, ended up conducting only four tutorials. All of Madeleine's tutorials occurred within three days of each other, in the sixth week of the quarter (Table 3-3; Note that the third of Madeleine's four sessions, detailed below, was singled out for analysis from the rest due to its atypical features). All four of Madeleine's recorded sessions dealt with four to six page major papers in which students were to make an argument involving articles on two views of multicultural education from Ronald Takaki's "A Different Mirror" and Arthur Slesinger's "The Return of the Melting Pot" and the English 105, or the second part of the stretch course, class they were taking. The sessions averaged 50 minutes, with the shortest lasting 31 minutes and the longest 71 minutes. Madeleine read the students' papers in the first two sessions aloud and she read them silently in the last two. I could not detect any noticeable effect this had on the content and flow of any of the sessions.

Madeleine evinced certain patterns in her tutoring practice that shaped the content and flow of the tutorials. Madeleine usually took control of the session early and held firm control of the conversational floor. Her sessions are characterized by little to no praise; plenty of criticism and directive suggestions, usually with no qualifications; and large chunks of time spent on talking, near-lecturing

Table 3-3: Linguistic features and cues from Madeleine's (Team Three) one-to-one tutorials

Linguistic Features and Cues	Madeleine	Students
# of Sessions	3/1	
Average Length (minutes)	50/59	
Total Words Spoken	12,115/7,614	1,919/2,997
Average # of Words Spoken per Minute	81/129	13/51
Content-clarifying Questions	5/4	
Open-ended Questions	23/2	
Directive Questions	23/5	
References to TA	7/4	0/2
References to Assignment Prompt	1/0	0/1
Interruptions	21/44	10/50
Main Channel Overlaps	3/6	7/25
Joint Productions	3/5	24/6

really, about the readings. The teacher, Sydney, plays an integral role in Madeleine's sessions. But Madeleine, rather than the students, brings the presence of Sydney into the session early on. This excerpt, from the beginning of the first tutorial, is typical of how Madeleine starts her sessions:

> MADELEINE: Okay looking at your introduction?
>
> STUDENT: Yeah introduction and claim.
>
> MADELEINE: And your claim. Is it okay if I read aloud?
>
> STUDENT: No go for it. MADELEINE READS STUDENT'S PAPER ALOUD FOR ABOUT TWO MINUTES
>
> MADELEINE: Okay I kind of see what you're trying to say. You're trying to say you're trying to set up the stakes like in the second paragraph? (yeah) You're trying to say that racism exists and the reason that racism exists is because people don't know about themselves (mmhhm). What I would say first of all about the beginning of your paper or the beginning paragraph is that it doesn't really have a claim that directly

> references both accounts (mmhmm) and maybe that's because you didn't have a copy of UNDECIPHERABLE
>
> STUDENT: Oh you mean the article?
>
> MADELEINE: Well first of all we're supposed to be talking about is multicultural education important? And you didn't really say anything about multicultural education in the beginning (oh) and so you just want to like mention that (okay). And also you're supposed to be stating whether or not you agree with the class that you just took. Like on race citizenship and the nation (ok). Like what she wants you to do is look at the class and think okay what have I gained from this class; like is it necessary for us to be studying these concepts or because the two different arguments are Takaki had his arguments well let's take the other guy first Sl- (Slesinger) JOINTPROD something hard to say. He basically says that multicultural education, it kind of like boosts people's self-esteem right?

Notice how after reading for a bit, Madeleine starts telling the student directly what the student is trying to say rather than ask her. Then Madeleine jumps straight into criticism of this student's introduction and claim without praising any aspect of the student's writing. She shows her close understanding of the assignment and implies an alignment with Sydney's expectations by telling the student, with the modal auxiliary, what she is "supposed" to be doing. Madeleine amplifies her alignment with Sydney and the prompt by bringing in the pronoun and presence of Sydney: "what *she* wants you to do." Madeleine typically uses the tag question "right?", as in the example here, not to necessarily elicit a student response as with an open-ended question, but (much like Julian) rather just to make sure that the student is following her suggestions. Madeleine goes on from the excerpt above to bring in Sydney via "she" twice more before she stops referring to her.

The above directive suggestions also in many ways parallel the third session, characterized by what I came to see as a struggle or fight for the conversational floor. This hour-long session involved so many overlaps by both interlocutors (92 interruptions, 16 joint productions, and 32 main channel overlaps) that it was quite painful to transcribe, even with voice-recognition software. This session is characterized by a student who fights for the conversational floor, especially in regards to the main concept she wants to cover in her essay, *politics*. The student brings up this issue as a possible focus for her claim early in the session and several times thereafter. But Madeleine ignores the idea repeatedly:

> STUDENT: I want to get out the thing is I have like three different things I'm trying to talk about (mm) and I don't know how to go at it; like I'm talking about how politically there are going to be more students educated and having a background of different peopleINTER
>
> MADELEINE: Yeah but I mean it's not just about it's not just about knowledge it's about knowledge of not only yourself like and how you fit into American history but how other groups not just black and white right? (yeah) fit into American history because Takaki one of his main arguments is also that American history has been really black-and-white like it's either white or it's the other (yeah) and the other is usually black. But that's not true because there's been like Latinos and there's been Asians and there's been Native Americans that have all helped to shape what America isINTER
>
> STUDENT: Yeah but what about because what I'm talking about here are the political process as a whole; like I actually take okay one of my positions is in a medical profession and the other one is a political position you know like what I'm saying? Okay I get the point that I'm not supposed to talk specifically about people going into the university and taking these courses and coming out a certain way, but that's kind of what I did. I'm talking about if you have a better understanding of each other there is going to be more laws formulated their going toINTER
>
> MADELEINE: But don't you think it's a little bit deeper than just having a better understanding likeINTER
>
> STUDENT: Well but that was that was deepINTER
>
> MADELEINE: Yeah but you're talking about he doesn't just say we need to like have a better understanding like try to use some of the terminology that he uses; one of the most important things that he says "we are influenced by which mirror we choose to see ourselves as" ...

> STUDENT: So the political one though I thought that would be okay; maybe I should just focus in on the student actually going into the schools oINTER
>
> MADELEINE: Well what you need to do is have an argument. So you agree with Takaki. Do you know what Takaki's claim is? (he) TEN SECOND PAUSE

This sort of conflict in goals continues until the student emotionally expresses her frustration in not being able to match Madeleine's insistence that she understand the texts (or *Madeleine's* interpretations of the texts):

> MADELEINE: I mean if you have to read it a couple more times INTER
>
> STUDENT: Well I'm trying to read a lot but it's just like I don't get what I'm doing though Madeleine ...

This is the first time a student has used Madeleine's name in any of the tutorial transcripts, an indication perhaps of the frustration that has been bottling up. Yet this is also the only time in *all* the tutorial transcripts I analyzed that a student called their tutor by name, suggesting a slightly more positive interpretation, perhaps, of the dramatic give and take of this interaction. Marie Nelson argued that the type of resistance this student evinces might actually suggest this student's potential to make dramatic progress because the resistance "showed how much students cared" (qtd. in Babcock and Thonus 91). This echoes Madeleine's own words regarding her motivation for this project: "I hoped that they would view my enthusiasm for the content as an example of it actually being cool to care."

Tellingly, *not one* comment regarding one-to-one tutorials came back from *student* questionnaires. Yet students had much to say about their in-class interactions with Madeleine, as readers will hear in the next chapter.

SURRENDERING CONTROL THROUGH THE ACT OF WRITING: SAM'S SESSIONS

Sam from **Team Four** was the tutor the least involved in any classroom activity. She was also expected to play the role of outside reader, or in her terms "independent consultant," in one-to-ones. Having less insider knowledge of the content of the course, and given Sam's typically nondirective approach, it would be reasonable to assume that Sam practiced a highly nondirective tutorial method with these students. Sam ended up conducting 11 tutorials total, eight sessions in the seventh week of the quarter, and three more in the tenth or final week (Table 3-4). All of Sam's sessions involved five to six page major papers. The first eight, including the tutorials detailed below, dealt with James Loewen's article on heroes and heroification, "Handicapped by History: The Process of Hero-Making." Since Sam had read most of the papers and supplied written comments beforehand, her sessions were designed to fit within a 30-minute time frame: the average session lasted 25 minutes, with the longest lasting 36 minutes and the shortest 16 minutes. Sam neither had students read papers aloud nor read them aloud for them.

Like the other tutors, Sam's tutorials began to show patterns early on that continued throughout her sessions. In contrast to Madeleine, Sam would usually start off by asking the students what they wanted to work on. This open-ended start would help set up Sam's habitual use of open-ended questions (OEQs) followed by follow-up questions and occasional directive or leading questions. Sam often used a praise-critique-suggestion sequence in her replies. Sam would qualify her suggestions much more often with phrases like "I would" or "I might" when nudging students toward acquisition of strategic knowledge. After the first few sessions, she began to say things like "I see a lot of students/people doing this" often when offering direct suggestions. Perhaps due to her more "outside reader" status, Sam referred back to the TA Sarah much less frequently than Megan, Julian, or Madeleine, instead using the phrase "the reader" to denote audience. In most of the papers, Sam talked about structure, the link between

Table 3-4: Linguistic features and cues from Sam's (Team Four) one-to-one tutorials

Linguistic Features and Cues	Sam	Students
# of Sessions	11	
Average Length (minutes)	25	
Total Words Spoken	18,181	11,292
Average # of Words Spoken per Minute	66	41
Content-clarifying Questions	20	
Open-ended Questions	137	
Directive Questions	21	
References to TA	1	3
References to Assignment Prompt	1	0
Interruptions	12	37
Main Channel Overlaps	7	12
Joint Productions	9	49

topic sentences and claim, between conclusion and claim. This often caused her to deal with sentence-level issues in relation to larger structural/rhetorical concerns. Finally, Sam's most salient and compelling patterns involved her use of note-taking and pauses and their overall effect on the content and flow of the tutorials. Sam's sophisticated use of note-taking and pauses caused students to talk much more than in Megan, Julian, or Madeleine's sessions, and led to what I would describe as collaborative speaking and writing *through the act of collaborative writing or note-taking.*

Sam began nine of her eleven sessions asking OEQs involving what the students wanted to work on: "Do you have any questions that you want to talk about?" is the typical way she opens up the tutorial. The two atypical openers in which Sam did not start in this way both started off with her asking about the students' claims. In the following excerpt, from the first round of tutorials, Sam evinces her typical praise-critique-suggestion pattern at the beginning of the tutorial:

> SAM: ... So it might be that you partly started reading the comments here but one of the things that I noticed about your paper is that you do a really good job of demonstrating your familiarity with all the material (mmhm). Like I can tell that you've done all the reading and paid close attention. What I think that you're missing though is a claim (mmhm) which is kind of a big part of writing an argumentative paper. So there's some scratch paper over there that you can take notes on if you want. But how I'd like to start is what what was your claim that you had in mind when you were working on the paper?

Even though Sam does not start off with her typical opener in this excerpt, she still begins with the broad OEQ regarding claim. More pointedly, in this session Sam begins to show her awareness of the importance of note-taking. In other sessions, she will ask students to take notes, while she takes notes as well. Sam's use of note-taking and pauses play the pivotal role in the content and flow of her tutorials, affecting not only how much students talk, but perhaps more importantly, *to what degree they take agency in the tutorial*—the number one factor that distinguishes her tutorials from all the ones conducted with the other teams.

In the following excerpt from a tutorial that lasted about 22 minutes, the student overlaps Sam's speech 12 times, while Sam does not overlap the student's *once.* The student is arguing that heroification is a bad influence on kids. Notice how pauses, questions, and overlaps function in the following extended excerpt:

SAM: Okay so you think SIX SECOND PAUSE so what's your take on heroification and how it affects little kids?

STUDENT: It helps to bias them, makes them makes them feel like you have to do the impossible SIX SECOND PAUSE the impossible by being perfect, having no flaws.

SAM: Okay so heroification is bad for kids to 16 SECOND PAUSE image, expectations.

STUDENT: Yeah it's just the image, what's right.

SAM: Okay and you said something about it rocks their mind with what do you mean by that?

STUDENT: The wrong example of what to do. 12 SECOND PAUSE

SAM: Okay, so why do you think that people do this? What did you understand from Loewen? Why do people try to hide the bad things? SEVEN SECOND PAUSE Why do you think people persist in presenting these unreal representations?

STUDENT: Just to do what they do now. They're trying to help. I have no idea why.

SAM: They're trying to helpJOINTPROD

STUDENT: Like kids try to be better. I mean that's FOUR SECOND PAUSE

SAM: Okay so heroification is meant to make kids be better. That you argue thatJOINTPROD

STUDENT: It doesn't do that.

SAM: Okay good. 22 SECOND PAUSE so if you were to sum that up into one statement because what we have here is it's not really something specific or arguable yet which is what a claim has to be. So if you were to sum up your ideas here in a statement one declarative statementINTER

STUDENT: So like tell why heroification is bad? (mmhm) Just because it gives the wrong ideas to kids on how to grow up.

SAM: Okay so would you write that in your paper and state it like that?

STUDENT: A lot like that. I don't know how I'd state it; it's easy to write down. I wouldn't say it's bad though. Heroification has a negative influence on kids because it gives them the wrong reasons to 43 SECOND PAUSE growing up it's negative for some kids TEN SECOND PAUSE the wrong reasons.

SAM: Well reasons for doing this. (yeah) Okay so that's good so I would just add that because this is yourINTER

STUDENT: In this sentence just get rid of this?

SAM: No leave this. This is a good transition here especially since you say that he focuses on high school. It still relates to kids; it just brings up the talk about kids which you do. Heroification has a negative influence on, etc.

STUDENT: So I can put this before the sentence?

SAM: I would put it hereJOINTPROD

STUDENT: After the sentence? Ok.

SAM: Because this is like your transitionJOINTPROD

STUDENT: So that'd move into myINTER(so it's) into that and I just want to this.

SAM: Yeah I would just kind of insert this here but then you have to talk about why you believe this is true.

STUDENT: So I would do that in the next paragraph? (so)

INTERor would I do that like in the same paragraph?

SAM: Well that's what the rest of your paragraph is about.
Basically you have to argue your point, make me believe you.
TEN SECOND PAUSE.

Sam begins with her typical OEQ. What the transcript does not reveal is that in the first long 16 second pause, Sam is writing notes. Sam has written something down, and then refers back to that in her follow-up question. Then Sam allows a 12 second pause after the student responds "the wrong example of what to do." After this pause, Sam asks more follow-up questions. When the student initially replies that she has "no idea why" and Sam begins to rephrase the student's beginning comments "they're trying to help," the student overlaps with a joint production, "like kids try to be better." In two more lines the student overlaps with another joint production. The next 22-second pause allows time for both participants to collect thoughts and get to the big picture, the claim. In the next few lines the student expresses the difficulty in trying to verbalize something as complex as wording the claim on the spot. But a few lines later a long 43 second followed closely by a ten-second pause allows the student to think more. The student interrupts Sam two lines later, expressing her concern at the sentence-level. Sam then explains through praise why she could keep that sentence and how it relates to the higher-order concerns involving structure and thesis: "This is a good transition here especially since you say that he focuses on high school. It still relates to kids it just brings up the talk about kids which you do heroification has a negative influence on, etc." The remainder of the excerpt above involves the student illustrating her agency by overlapping Sam's speech three more times—two of which she actually interrupts Sam's attempt to respond. Notice how the line between interruption and joint production begins to slightly blur when the conversation is really flowing, when the student is realizing some agency and urgency, and when the tutor (Sam) allows for this sort of conversational play. (During initial transcriptions, I had some difficulty in distinguishing between interruptions and joint productions in some spots.)

Sam's longest session evinces many of the same patterns described above, further illustrating the collaborative effects of Sam's particular style. During analysis, I was struck by how similar this student was to the one that Madeleine from Team Three had such conversational struggle with in her session above. In this 36 minute session, the student overlaps Sam's speech 20 times, while Sam only overlaps the student's speech five times—including three instances where the student *does not* allow Sam to take control of the conversational floor. In this session Sam shows one of her patterns early in the tutorial when she says "So one problem that a lot of people have tends to be coming up with the claim in the beginning." Sam refers to what she notices that others have been doing often, perhaps deflecting any sort of individualized, evaluative finger-pointing. The student starts off describing his claim as involving his belief that heroification is ok for young kids, but that when they start to mature they need to be able to think critically about this issue. Sam proceeds to ask questions and provide suggestions on how the student can rethink his topic sentences in relation to his claim. In typical fashion, she qualifies most of her suggestions, "When you're revising I'd probably, what I recommend ..." Discussion of the essay's structure leads to a discussion of the student's prewriting strategies. Later the conversation turns back to more specific instances of getting the student's purposes across clearly to the reader. Here Sam shows her typical reference to the reader: "So all that's really needed is that you want to make sure that you specifically say this at the beginning of this paragraph (oh ok) so that we know that that's what you're saying. (oh ok) So that we know that as we read the scene we go 'okay so this is where he's going with this.'"

A few turns later, the student second-guesses himself when he feels that Sam has disagreed with one of his points:

> STUDENT: ... That was just like me presenting both sides of the argument; but clearly, like I'm thinking maybe it doesn't belong because you're telling me like okay this UNDECIPHERABLE.
>
> SAM: Okay so do you feel like this fits in with any of your major points so far? Sorry I didn't have a good look at the first paragraph should beJOINTPROD
>
> STUDENT: More of a benefit really.
>
> SAM: Or yeah what was the first body paragraph?
>
> STUDENT: It was more like morale of like heroification can be used to build up morale. To want to be great you don't need to hear the negative sides to put a high standard upon yourself; I guess that was kind of it. We could just move that chunk overINTER(well ok)
>
> SAM: So let's think about this, you've got heroification can build up morale, but then if it gets too blown up out of proportion then there's a danger that it will break down and fail because it's a lie. (mmhm) And then the third danger is

> that those that are deceived won't be able to UNDECIPEH-RABLE what they're thinking. So of those three which do you think it fits better with?
>
> STUDENT: Definitely more on the benefit. Well I'm not really sure because that part of my argument was more like I realize I was more focused on possibilities and I kinda wanted to end on a little bit of both because it shows that kinda gave two sides but mainly push towards one thing whether something good can come out of it if you're going to set yourself for the challenge.

In contrast to the fight-for-the-floor pace and tone of Madeleine's third tutorial, in this excerpt and throughout this and all of her sessions, Sam takes a much less argumentative (doubting, dissenting) and much more cooperative (believing, assenting) stance in relation to the student's ideas. Notice how precisely Sam refers back to the student's ideas and words:

> So let's think about this. You've got heroification can build on morale, but then if it gets too blown out of proportion then there's a danger that it will break down and fail because it's a lie. (mmhm) And then the third danger is that those that are deceived won't be able to UNDECIPHERABLE what they're thinking. So of those three which do you feel it fits better with?

Because Sam has been writing notes, co-constructing an outline with the student, she can repeat back, with some great detail and clarity, the student's own ideas and how they relate to the overall essay. The student then can help add to this co-constructed oral/literate text. This exemplifies what I would describe as collaborative speaking and writing *through the act* of synergistic writing or note-taking.

Rather than dismiss any of the student's ideas, or try to force ideas on the student (as Madeleine, Julian, and Megan were all prone to do sometimes) Sam uses questions to try to get at how this student's idea might be worked into the essay's structure. This reliance on traditionally nondirective questions is due to some degree to the fact that Sam has not done the course readings. But it is also due, I believe, to Sam's methodology. Sam's tenacious ability to stick to using questions to allow students time to process and respond and then to write down notes as the conversation moves forward as her basic "nondirective" modus operandi enables her to turn the conversation over to the hands and minds of the students. In one session Sam waited for *89 seconds* after asking a student

"So where's your topic sentence on this paragraph"? That same student, after thinking through things for 89 seconds, responded in some detail. While tutors are typically advised to wait fifteen seconds for a reply before reframing the question, some questions may require longer cognitive processing. Courtney Cazden, drawing on Hugh Mehan, claims these "*metaprocess* questions ask for different kinds of knowledge and prompt longer and more complex responses" (46). While "what is your topic sentence?" may seem simple enough on the surface, imagine all the cognitive steps the student must go through to give a cogent reply: processing the question, putting the question of how the topic for one area of the paper relates to the larger structure of the rest of the paper, and finally trying to find the words to express those connections. This moves the student simultaneously from the larger rhetorical-structural issues of the paper to the micro-linguistic syntactical and lexical level of the topic sentence. Each student that Sam worked with walked away with jointly-constructed notes that they could use while revising their essays.

Of the 12 *student* questionnaires I received, ten were overwhelmingly positive and only two were either critical or ambivalent. (The ambivalent one was from a student who did not visit Sam in the first place.) Most students commented on the convenience of the partnership and the availability of Sam. Students described specifically how helpful Sam was during one-to-ones. For example, one student wrote: "It helped me strengthen my paper and understand what the readings were trying to get across to its audience." Another, "She gave me ideas and hints to making my paper be voiced more by me rather than the quotes I used." Another, "She helped me gather my thoughts clearly, gave me advice to make my paper stronger." Two students commented favorably on Sam commenting on their papers before they met: "we would go to our appointment and she would have our paper already read so we didn't have to wait. She would just tell us what we had to work on." Another, "It was a lot better because at least the tutor would read it beforehand and it would not take as long as opposed to making an appointment or a drop-in where they would read it on the spot and it would take a while." Finally, one student commented on what she saw as a problem, suggesting what some students must think of writing centers in general: "The tutor was not familiar with the subject taught in class; therefore she wasn't able to help on specific questions or be any more helpful than the tutors at the writing center."

DISCUSSION: TUTORING ON THE EDGE OF EXPERTISE

Granted, the case studies represent extremes in tutorial instruction and tutor preparation and should only be taken for what they truly are, qualitative case studies conducted in local contexts. Yet, analyzed side-by-side (Appendix C)—and from so many methodological angles—they suggest multiple points for more general comparative consideration, especially in regards to tutoring method. While CBT scholars caution practitioners and experimenters that tutors may need to be more or less directive when interacting more closely with instructors and courses, my studies suggest just how tricky this notion really is.

Julian's (**Team One**) basic modus operandi of having the student read the paper aloud, while stopping intermittently to talk about things as they went, seemed to cause Julian to talk unnecessarily, and in ways that only occasionally invited students to take agency in the sessions. Julian made infrequent use of the valuable tool of note-taking, a technique that might have substantially altered the content and flow of his one-to-ones. If he had asked his questions, then waited for a response, then taken notes for the students (especially those that were not as engaged or not taking any notes themselves) his sessions may have sounded more like Sam's, and students and Anne may have felt that these one-to-ones were adding something of value to this partnership. Instead, Julian—despite his meta-awareness that he tends to talk too much (listen too little) in a tutorial—repeatedly dominated the conversational floor, often interrupting students' train of thought, answering the questions he should have been waiting for a response on, and even out-and-out ignoring (or more often, overlooking) student concerns and questions. Stunningly, during our interview, Julian even told me that he felt the one-to-one tutorials were "successful."

When held in comparison to Megan and Kim, however, Julian's style does not seem that drastically different or reprehensible. In fact, all three of these tutors exhibited similar tendencies to dominate much of the conversational floor in their own ways. (Students actually talked more, proportionately, with Julian than with Megan or Kim.) Julian, unfortunately did not have the same opportunity as the in-class tutors to redeem himself in any way via consistent and productive interactions in the classroom. (I'll return to this comparative discussion in the next chapter.)

Megan's (**Team Two**) tutorials took two different routes: shorter sessions in which she did almost all of the talking, asked few questions, and followed her usual pattern of praise-critique-suggestion; and longer sessions in which students, concerned with negotiating their portfolios or Laura's comments, showed more engagement and concern, but still talked much less. These shorter sessions resemble the kind of conferences advocated by Garrison, shorter sessions where the tutor/teacher acts more like an editor directly intervening and offering suggestions. In a sample session with a student, Garrison often uses phrases like "this is what I would do" or more emphatically "do this" or "I want you to." He will even ask the student a question, then, rather than wait for a response, move on to the next question or suggestion or critique (see Harris, *Teaching One-to-One* 143-45). In the excerpt Harris cites, Garrison does not praise, but moves quickly from critique to critique. In contrast, Megan follows a pattern of praise-critique-suggestion that students must certainly be familiar with from teacher end-comments on their papers, and perhaps even from peer review. Drawing on Aristotle's idea of praise as action, Spigelman argues that students in classroom writing groups need to be taught the value of both epideictic and deliberative rhetorical responses. "In contrast to epideictic," she writes,

> an exclusionary deliberative approach may ... contribute to wholesale reader appropriation with little concern for writer's intentions or motives ... When groups believe that their primary function is to change the existing text, they may fail to notice and therefore positively reinforce successful literary or rhetorical elements in their peer's essays ... A combined epideictic and deliberative process enables readers to provide productive, action-oriented comments, and at the same time, allows writers to resist appropriation by their peers ("'Species'" 147-8).

While it is important to praise for several reasons (Daiker; Harris, *Teaching One-to-One* 71-73), some maintain that too much lavish praise may have little positive, and perhaps even a slightly negative, effect on student learning (see Schunk 475-6). As I listened to Megan's use of praise repeatedly in both peer reviews and one-to-ones, I began to wonder if it was having the effect on students she intended. Megan's praise, however, did sound more authentic when she aligned her praise with Laura's. This associative "team praising" allowed Megan to amplify her praise considerably, affectively easing the worries of students who perhaps felt there was little worth celebrating in Laura's comments and evaluations. Megan also evinced a willingness to help students with sentence- and word-level issues. Megan's transcripts show how a tutor willing to work through sentence- and word-level concerns can immediately link these issues back to HOCs like claim, especially the important role of word choice and carefully defining terms so that a writer can get their intended point across to their reader more clearly. Finally, we saw how Megan's sessions took a different turn when it came time for students to negotiate their portfolio assignment at the end of the quarter. When students perceive the stakes as high, and I would argue, when they are dealing with the unfamiliar genre of the portfolio cover letter, they take a much more active role in the tutorial. Megan's sessions began to involve exploratory talk much more, it seems, when the students felt the real urgency involved in arguing the strengths and weaknesses of their performance for the course.

We also saw in Megan's first round of sessions that she started off with a typically non-directive approach, but soon, as she progressively worked with more and more students, she became increasingly directive, more Garrison-like. Most likely, seeing students with the same assignment repeatedly, caused Megan to start blurring each session together, almost into one huge tutorial. This is much less likely to happen in a typical one-to-one tutorial outside of CBT.

Madeleine (from **Team Three**) proved a highly directive tutor. As we discussed at length in Chapter Two, directive tutoring does not necessarily imply hierarchical, authoritarian tutoring. For my analyses here (and also in relation to Madeleine's in-class involvement discussed in the next chapter), it is worth noting that Madeleine evinces conversational and instructional communication patterns associated with African Americans, patterns that may account in part for her instructional directiveness (see Delpit *Other*; Smitherman; Lee; Denny 42-43). Carol Lee, drawing on Bakhtin, Goffman, and Geneva Smitherman, points especially to AAVE as a personal discourse that brings special ways of speaking and knowing into the classroom (and, for our purposes, into one-to-one and small-group tutorials): "Within AAVE (which may be defined as a dialect of English), there are many speech genres. These genres include, but are not limited to, signifying, loud talking, marking, and testifying" (131). She draws on Smitherman's *Talk that Talk* to explain how the African-American communicative-rhetorical tradition evinces some unique patterns:

1. Rhythmic, dramatic, evocative language
2. Reference to color-race-ethnicity
3. Use of proverbs, aphorisms, Biblical verses
4. Sermonic tone reminiscent of traditional Black church
5. Use of cultural referents and ethnolinguistic idioms
6. Verbal inventiveness, unique nomenclature
7. Cultural values—community consciousness
8. Field dependency (involvement with and immersion in events and situations; personalizing phenomena; lack of distance from topics and subjects) (Smitherman, 2000, p., 186)

Madeleine evinced especially 1, 2, 5, 7, and 8 in her tutorials, partly (perhaps largely) because the topic of the course—race and citizenship in the nation—brought out her passion and fluency on this topic (also see Corbett, Lewis, and Clifford). In "Community, Collaboration, and Conflict" Evelyn Westbrook reports on an ethnography of a community writing group where conflict and difference are foregrounded. One group member, an African-American woman (echoing Lisa Delpit's direct-instruction sentiments), rather than placing the highest value on supporting its members through lavish epideictic praise, sees more value in challenging its members:

> when people [in the group] say "Wow! This is good," well, that doesn't help me very much. But when they say, "I would use this or I would use that" or when they challenge the way I thought about [something], that's good feedback ... When someone questions something you do as a writer ... they are really saying, "Make me understand this." (238)

While readers might understandably question Madeleine's performance during one-to-one tutorials, in the next chapter I'll report on the degree to which that same authoritative style was evinced and speculate on how effective and valuable it proved to students in the classroom.

Nondirective methods and moves were showcased by Sam (from **Team Four**) in all of her one-to-one tutorials. But I might critique Sam's performances in two ways. First, almost every move Sam made during her one-to-ones placed agency on the tutee. She asked many open-ended and follow-up questions. She took careful and detailed notes, to which she and the students added to and referred back to during the course of the tutorials (see Harris, *Teaching One-to-One* 108; Gillespie and Lerner 74). She allowed for long, extended, patient pauses that aided tremendously in both the students' and her abilities to process information and formulate responses and questions. She also—like Megan from Team Two evinced throughout both her one-to-one tutorials and during peer response facilitation and so *unlike* Madeleine—used praise strategically. Yet, I might also say that the model Sam employed (at the specific request of Sarah) necessarily caused her to deploy the methods she did. Because she was less in-the-know, because she did not know as much of the content and flow of the day-to-day course happenings, and because she was trained to approach tutorials primarily from a nondirective methodology (and, recall, actually worried about being too directive), Sam was much more situated to practice a nondirective method. This method caused her to deploy such strategically valuable methods as almost always starting sessions by asking what the student wanted to work on, using a praise-critique-suggestion conversational sequence, referring to general "readers" rather than to the instructor Sarah or to the assignment, and thoughtfully and patiently crafting notes. We might, then, say that—like the successful tutorials we surveyed in Chapter One from White-Farnham, Dyehouse, and Finer, and Thompson—Sam realized the coveted humble/smart balance.

Since Sam and Sarah from **Team Four** had the least amount of in-class interaction with each other of all the teams, I will provide some details of their own reflections of their partnership here. The data point to an overall highly successful partnership. Since Sam did not attend any classes in an instructional role, she primarily voices how she and Sarah coordinated their activities out of class, and the effects these communications had on Sam's involvement with students:

> My involvement with the TA was pretty minimal. We mostly contacted each other via email. I saw her a couple of times, but not really during the quarter. She mostly sent me the prompts and we emailed each other. I'd give her my availability and she would send that to the class. They'd sign up for appointments and then she would send their sign-ups to me.

Sam said that at first she was a little worried that she wasn't involved enough with the students, but from what she was hearing from Sarah noted "I think it turned out pretty well." Sam and Sarah even agreed from the start that it would be better if Sam did not do any of the course readings. Sam suggests a fear of being too directive: "I thought it would be more helpful to go with the prompt with their papers ... because I might have my own ideas on where they should be taking their papers and I wanted to avoid that. I just wanted to help them bring out their own claims and arguments." And although Sam did not have any in-class interaction with students, she did feel a closer connection and responsibility to these students:

> I felt more tied to the success of the students in this class. I really wanted them to do better. I wanted Sarah to see the improvements in their papers. I wanted to help them get more out of the class as a whole. And I think that comes with being connected to a particular class. It makes you more invested.

Sam pointed to this as a reason why she would have liked to have had closer interaction with Sarah and the class. She spoke of establishing a more definite sense of her role in the course. She talked about coming in earlier to explain to the students her role. And she said it would have been better if she had spoken with Sarah more about how the class was going, or even visited the classroom once or twice, "just maybe coming in and sitting in the back a couple of times, letting them know you're there and you're tied to the class rather than some loner from the outside."

Sarah provides further insight into Team Three's unique partnership, including Sam's minimal involvement with certain aspects of the course. Overall, Sarah really enjoyed the partnership. Like most participants, she said she greatly appreciated the convenience of having a specific tutor readily available for students to make appointments with. Sarah said she wanted Sam to play the role of peer tutor and outside reader for the class, rather than co-teacher: "I might've been uncomfortable having another person in the classroom, but that might just be my own ego [laughter]. Seriously though, one of my other concerns too is that students might be confused having too many authority figures." Sarah decided not to have Sam do the readings because she was afraid that "the tutor would know all the readings that we're doing and would know the kinds of arguments I'm looking for, and they might steer the students in that direction." Of course, this is exactly what we saw Madeleine attempting to do in her tutorials.

I maintain, however, that even if Madeleine had been exposed to the literature on nondirective tutoring—like Julian and Megan, who had more experience and training—she still would have experienced the same type of conflicts in agency and authority she faced in attempting to help students negotiate the course. (This may have even conflicted more strikingly with her perhaps more directive African-American instructional style as we discussed above.) Although Madeleine's four tutorials is quite a small data set, my experiences and case-study research over the years as well as the literature on CBT strongly suggest that tutors faced with a tutorial situation in which they have a better understanding of the course content, teacher expectations, and perhaps even closer interpersonal relationships with the students, will face a tougher challenge negotiating between directive and nondirective tutorial methods. But I do not believe this is necessarily a bad thing, nor should it deter us from continuing to practice CBT. I would rather continue to encourage tutors (and instructors) to practice at the edge of their pedagogical expertise and interpersonal facility. More specifically, for CBT and for consideration of CBT and tutors who have more or less training or experience, how might we, and why should we, encourage tutors to reap the benefits of both directive and nondirective tutoring strategies?

If a tutor has the confidence and motivation to connect more closely with a writing classroom and help provide a strong model of academic communication and conversation—regardless of how much formal training they've received—should we be open to such teaching and learning partnerships? In the next chapter, I'll present what can happen when tutors make these expeditions, interacting with instructors and students in the classroom. Sam (and Sarah's) narrative of success has all but been concluded. But will vociferous Julian and Madeleine (and to a degree Megan) prove more relatively effective in the classroom than they did in their one-to-ones? And what about those tutors from SCSU who played all of their tutorial roles strictly in the classroom? In many ways, their dramas have yet to unfold ....

CHAPTER FOUR

CONFLICT AND CARE WHILE TUTORING IN THE CLASSROOM: CASE STUDIES AT THE UNIVERSITY OF WASHINGTON AND SOUTHERN CONNECTICUT STATE UNIVERSITY

> On occasion, a person with a marginalized identity gains confidence to persist in the face of prevailing winds that trumpet convention.
>
> – Harry Denny

> Now is the time for peripheral visions.
>
> – Jackie Grutsch McKinney

In this chapter I extend the work of fellow course-based tutoring researchers by offering detailed comparisons, drawn from my field notes and interviews, as we inch increasingly closer to an understanding of the many factors that provoke directive and nondirective tutoring strategies and that can encourage or deter successful CBT classroom interactions. Rebecca Babcock and Terese Thonus draw on research from the California State University Fresno Writing Center to argue, in contrast to one-to-one tutorials, "the validity of tutoring groups as an effective, and even superior, means of supporting basic writers" (92). I agree with this claim, but I also believe it warrants continuing scrutiny. What factors might make for successful classroom interactions? How can tutors best facilitate and support small-group peer response sessions in the developmental writing classroom? And what useful connections can be drawn between one-to-one and small-group tutoring in CBT situations?

I start my reporting and analyses with case studies of tutors involved in peer response facilitation in the classrooms they were connected to. I'll begin with the three teams from the UW that were actively involved in the classroom. In the first subsection, I offer detailed micro-analyses of four tutor-led peer response sessions. These sessions are unique and worth micro-analyses due to the fact that both tutors, Julian and Megan, were trained to adhere to a more nondirective tutoring method and methodology. Their performances, then, when compared to their one-to-ones from Chapter Three, aid in my efforts to draw connections between the discourses of one-to-one and small-group tutoring. In the second subsection, I turn my reporting and analyses toward the teams with tutors who received no explicit training in directive/nondirective strategies. Rather than focusing on the micro-level language of the interactions, I focus my analyses more peripherally, more on the broader rhetorical actions and attitudes of the participants. All in all, readers will hear detailed, multivocal and multi-perspectival analyses of tutors—some of whom we've already seen deep in action—with varying levels of experience and training and widely different personalities and preconceived notions attempt to aid fellow students with their writing performances on location in the classroom.

CONNECTING THE MICRO AND MACRO IN PEER RESPONSE FACILITATION: TEAMS ONE AND TWO

Redemption Song or Cautionary Tale? Julian on Location

I thought for sure—had complete trust—that Julian and Anne of **Team One** would realize a fruitful partnership. Just glancing at the highly positive student course evaluations for the course overall, one would never get a sense that things were not all they could have been with that partnership. Yet, as we clearly saw from our analyses of one-to-one tutorial transcripts, Julian confounded my (and students') expectations. Surely, he fared better in the classroom. The following scenarios take readers closer to an understanding of how authority, trust and directive/nondirective method negotiation can intertwine to either deter or promote successful peer response facilitation.

What follows are reports and analyses of peer response sessions facilitated by Julian and Anne on two different days drawn from my field notes. Due to the dynamic nature of multiple speakers in small groups, I have opted for a horizontal transcription style:

> In the first peer review session, in week five, eight students are in attendance, arranged in two groups of four. I move to Julian's group. He asks if people brought extra copies. A student replies: "Only one." First student starts to read his paper. Other students are listening, but not writing, commenting or taking notes yet. Julian jots notes as the student continues read-

ing. Student One says: "Didn't catch your claim." Student Two says: "Should be in your introduction." The writer points it out and rereads it. Julian asks: "What do you all think of that as a claim?" Student Two says: "Sounds more like your opinion." Julian says: "Consider bringing in extra copies [of their essays]. Student One says: "None of us knew there was peer editing today." Julian says (commenting on the writer's paper): "Notes on logos, pathos, ethos; good intertextuality; citings of Takaki; with the claim feels like something's missing, stakes; could you read it again?" The writer re-reads the claim. Julian asks: "Why is it important?" Writer repeats the second part of the claim with some extra commentary. Julian says: "That sounds good, that would give the stakes." Student One says: "Could state whether or not you agree with Takaki." The writer asks: "What about opinions?" Julian answers: "The idea is the whole paper is your opinion; stating opinions as if they are a fact, sorta like tricking your reader that your opinion is fact." *Julian asks the student reviewers:* "Patterns in a section that you did?" Student Two says: "Logos, cause he keeps giving facts, then the stakes, then facts." Julian says: "It seems it might not be too much more work to find the pattern. If there isn't a pattern, that might be worth commenting on." Julian asks the writer: "Any particular questions?" This group continues in similar fashion. (At this point I notice Anne has stayed primarily out of the groups. She spent about ten minutes with the other group, then she went to her desk for about ten minutes, then came back to the group.)

Julian moves on to the next group. The group he leaves continues talking on-task. In the next group a writer is in the middle of reading his paper aloud. Julian listens quietly. The writer is catching and commenting on many of his own mistakes as he reads aloud. Julian says: "That's one of the advantages of reading aloud; can catch your own mistakes." The group members agree verbally and with head shakes. Student One says: "Sounds like you're making a list; really choppy." Group members again verbally and nonverbally assent. Julian says: "I missed the beginning; what is the claim?" The writer says: "What is a real American? She claims only white people are true Americans." *Julian asks the reviewers*: "What stands

> out as the stakes for his claim?" Student One says: "Word choice, tone." Student 2, overlapping his response with Student 1, says: "Go into more depth about Asian Americans." The bell rings and the session ends.

What I find most interesting about both these peer review groups is how Julian actually does seem to be fulfilling his role as peer review facilitator when he prompts (in italics) students to comment on each other's papers (much as Megan from Team Two does below), and the degree to which Julian tries to stay as closely as possible to the assignment prompt in his suggestions. Notice in both groups how Julian emphasizes claim, stakes, patterns, and the rhetorical appeals—all things detailed in the assignment prompt. On their perception of how the session went, both Anne and Julian agreed that students should have been told to bring in extra copies. (Each student brought only one paper copy.) Although Anne felt this was "probably not my best peer review session ever," she liked how the opening discussion of the ground rules and strategies for peer review got the students involved early in the shaping of the session and gave them an understanding of why they were doing things the way they were. "In the name of metacognition, you know," she said. Julian felt that while there were some good things that occurred, "overall I don't think it went very well." Julian blamed it primarily on not having extra essay copies, and also on a lack of time, but also pointed to what he felt was a problem with the assignment prompt: "There were so many bold words/ideas on their essay prompt, they didn't seem to really know what to be talking about. None of the students seemed comfortable or fully in control of all the discipline-specific language, i.e., there was no common parlance amongst the peer group for all the essay's aspects in discussion."

> In the second small-group peer response session I observed a few weeks later, Julian only worked with one group of two students the entire time. The main thing I noticed about this session was that, besides reading aloud, the students barely spoke at all during the entire roughly forty minutes. The frustrating effect this had on Julian was palpable to me and must have seemed so to the students as well. Near the beginning of the session Julian asks Student One if he is comfortable reading aloud. Student One says "not really." Julian describes why it is a good idea to read aloud: "It helps everyone stay in the same place, and you might hear and catch many of your own mistakes." Without answering, Student One proceeds to read his paper aloud. Julian cuts in quickly and asks if he can slow down, that he "can't process what he's saying." Student

> One slows down considerably. As the student continues to read Anne writes more instructions on the board: "Is there a controlling thread of argument about what the readers need to take away from these texts? Is it persuasive? What would you say is at stake? Are all sources appropriately cited? Do the content, structure, evidence, appeals, tone all keep the reader in mind?"
>
> What follows, to me, is Julian's attempt to help students juggle all the well-intentioned prompting Anne has provided. I would call the resulting session an example of "resource overload," or more is less. As in the peer review session above, Julian spent the entire session mostly trying to get these two students to talk about how they could get one of Anne's prompt items, "Content," working in their texts. There was no mention, nor any attempts at working another prompt item "Creative" textual potentialities into the conversation. Reflecting on this session, Julian felt it went poorly. He felt the groups were too small to encourage much comparative discussion. He also felt that perhaps students did not fully understand the assignment which, along with their unwillingness to talk about "their own writing process (or lack thereof)," left him with little to discuss. He said that although the two students hadn't really done the assignment they "professed to understand what the assignment was." Anne did not offer any reflections on this particular session.

Although Julian felt it was overall a good thing that he did attend the two peer review sessions, his explanations of the role he sees himself playing during peer review points to possible reasons why he experienced such lackluster results. Ironically, it just might be Julian's sophisticated sense of what he *should* be doing during peer response that contributed to the problem. Keenly aware of authority issues, Julian feels that his role in peer review is one of "reserved adviser." He elaborates:

> My understanding is that my presence during the peer critique sessions, it's not a tutoring session, it's not me working one-on-one trying to work with their particular writing issues. It's me trying to model for them skills and ways of being effective in future peer groups throughout their writing classes and college careers, so that they can be useful to other people

when I'm not around.

He spoke of previous peer review experiences, among the many he had participated in, where he had taken a more directive approach and felt that this causes students to "clam up because it stops becoming a peer critique session because I'm not their peer anymore and the whole process breaks down and becomes something other than what it's intended to be." Julian felt that the biggest roadblock to success, however, involved lack of regular communication between him and Anne.

Rather than share the blame, as Julian did above, Anne, more than once, intimated how she should have done a better job scheduling conferences, getting Julian course materials, and most of all "including Julian in sort of the day-to-day workings of the class and making sure that he had sort of a well-defined role." She goes on to explain how she feels this communicative oversight later caused students to have expectations of the sort of help they would receive from Julian that were never met. One of these expectations may have involved how much direct instruction they thought they might receive from Julian. Anne talked at length about how Julian's nondirective approach made her reconsider this approach in relation to this group of developmental students. She said that she had hoped that Julian might help disrupt her teacherly authority somewhat. She felt that because Julian was trying so hard to stay within what he thought were her expectations, he forfeited any opportunity for students to really stake their own claims, something she would have valued highly: "They're the quickest to bow to authority. They're the quickest to say 'well am I doing it right?' And the least likely in some ways to sort of say 'I don't think that's a useful way of approaching this question' or 'what can we do with this assignment to make it something real for me and not just some imagined scenario or something.'"

Three *students* mentioned peer review in their course evaluations, one praising, the others critical. The first student, pointed to both her admiration of Anne, and the value she saw in peer review: "Anne is an amazing professor and it seems like she absolutely loves what she does and it makes me want to learn more from her. Peer review also played a big role when writing difficult papers. It's always nice to bounce ideas off your peers and contribute in making their papers better." The second student, however, felt "we spent too much time reading each other's paper[s] during peer review, leaving no time for comments ... Taking each other's papers home to read before the actual day of peer review [would have improved the peer review process]" The third student, commenting on what aspects of the class detracted from his/her learning, wrote two words: "peer reviews."

Peer Review People: Megan on Location

Megan, from **Team Two**, felt she was acting much more like a peer in the classroom than a teacher, and she saw this as a good thing. She evinced to me that she worried she would become "more of the TA or assistant TA and not the tutor." She goes on to explain that she was relieved when other, less authoritative roles were agreed upon between her and Laura. But Megan elaborated further about role negotiation, especially what exactly her role was supposed to be in the classroom:

> We didn't have too many class discussions so I wasn't really a discussion leader. I tried to ask questions that would really help them understand the readings. But I guess I was kind of peer review [laughter] person. I would lead peer review at times and kind of help them with a new way to do that ... and not much else actually I guess.

Both of the peer review sessions I observed for Team Two seemed to involve both Megan and Laura in dynamic peer review and response facilitation and instruction with the entire class:

> For the first peer review, in the third week, 12 students are in attendance. Laura assigns four students to three groups, writing the group assignments on the board. She reminds them that they are supposed to have two copies. Laura has Megan come to the front and explain how the peer review session will work: decide who goes first, read your essay aloud, go through the worksheet, note things that don't make sense. Megan says that Laura and she will go from group to group. Laura passes around the peer review sheet, and explains that these sheets should be attached to their essays when turned in. Next, Megan and Laura each attach themselves to a separate group. In Megan's group students begin to fill out the review sheets as the first writer reads his paper. Megan takes notes. Upon finishing reading, Megan says that he did really well and asks for observations from fellow group members. Student One says "Nice examples. It would be nice if you could include some quotes to bring out details." Megan replies "Good suggestion." Student Three says "Good flow." Student Four follows with "flow nice." Megan says "Introduction describing surveillance knew what you would be talking about ... the other responders gave good advice ... In academics I was hoping to hear a little more about surveillance in your social life and during the games ... Who is surveilling you? Be careful

> about 'being watched,' word choice, maybe 'surveilled' ... details help make your points really clear; excellent, good job!" Megan certainly seems to be the authority figure here. She talks much more than the other students, who seem reluctant to offer any suggestions.
>
> Writer Two reads his paper aloud. Fellow group members jot down notes. (Laura is still attached to the first group, listening, giving feedback apparently as a group member. Then she moves to the other group, listening, answering a few questions about the peer review sheet.) Megan says "Why don't we do the same thing ... you want to go first? The level of student involvement picks up a little in this next round of responses. Student One offers some advice to the writer regarding his paper: "another suggestion, lack of style ... maybe make it more interesting ... I might make it like a story, rather than explaining steps." The writer seems unsure, slightly resistant (non-verbally mostly), to this suggestion. After group members discuss what they believe is the writer's claim and offer a few more suggestions, Megan says "It was a good job. I'm going to the next group; just continue as you're doing."
>
> At this group (the first Laura was at; now she is at the third group) a student is reading aloud; other students are taking notes; one asks for clarification during reading. Megan takes notes on what she hears. Rather than Megan, Student One starts the response: "Good, explain what panopticon is." Student Two says: "Good structure, describing and comparing to panopticon; but would be nice to describe activity." Student One agrees. Megan says: "That's a good observation." One more student comments, then Megan takes over the conversation for the rest of the class period, ending with: "You guys did a great job; sometimes students don't. I've been in classrooms where it's like pulling teeth to get them to." A student asks if Megan is still taking classes. They start to chat about her classes, future plans in teaching, etc. He asks her questions; other members in the group join in; conversation is casual and friendly.

Within days of this session, I solicited Megan and Laura for their impressions of how things went. Laura said that she had asked students how it went and she got back mixed reviews. Some students said the oral peer review style made it difficult to correct grammatical errors. Some said that reading the papers aloud helped them to recognize the structure of their papers. Laura wished she had had one tutor for each group. Megan said that by reading aloud, she felt students caught a lot of their own mistakes. She also commented on how many of these students had the first part of this stretch-course together and she believes this allowed them to feel comfortable and to be open and honest with each other. She had interesting things to say about the peer review sheets:

> I think that the peer review sheets were helpful, but sometimes unnecessary. In group two I think they were doing what I would hope would happen in a peer review session, but they were not filling in their sheets as much. Whereas in group one they all filled in the sheets while the person was reading the paper aloud and then talked about the suggestions they had for the paper. I think that both were effective, but I think that sometimes students can get distracted with filling in the sheet and not giving the best feedback. For this reason, I would not have a peer review sheet. However, I can see how it might have been effective. Who knows, if there was not a worksheet in group one, they might have not paid as close attention and thus not had as many insightful comments. However, I think that group two did a wonderful job and may not get that acknowledgment because they did not fill in their worksheets as completely as group one. It is a tough balance.

It is clear to see that students were caught between what Laura called the "oral peer review" and the peer review that relied on filling out the sheet she had used with most of these students. While Megan was encouraging verbal conversation in her groups, Laura was emphasizing filling out the worksheet: "I instructed the first group I worked with step by step. We answered most of the questions on the peer review sheet. I gave less instruction to the second group, because when I got there they already figured out a different way of doing oral peer review."

Four weeks later I was invited to their second peer review session. It seems as if they had made a couple of adjustments from the first one:

> Less students end up showing up for this session, nine overall, divided into two groups. Laura chooses a group leader for group one and has that leader choose who she wants for the group. Laura then passes around the peer review sheet (a different one) and says, however, that she wants them to talk

> about their papers first. Megan goes to group one, Laura to group two. Having a group leader somewhat changes the dynamics of group one's session. The group leader initiates questions and prompts speakers. But Megan soon resumes her role as authority figure by offering suggestions liberally; she ends up doing over half of the talking. However, having a different group leader than the implied Megan did seem to involve students more in the flow of the conversation, suggestions offered and questions asked, than the first group Megan worked with above.
>
> The second group stands out in my memory and field notes for the way students seemed to control much more of the conversational floor. At right about the half-way point Megan and Laura switch groups. The flow of conversation seems strong and students readily offer answers to Megan's prompting questions. But the conversation becomes really dynamic as Megan asks the writer about her paper. The writer talks about her paper on Britney Spears. Megan asks about sources. The writer says none. *Megan asks if anyone can suggest texts/sources for her.* Student Two suggests Foucault and why. Megan summarizes her words. Student Four chimes in. Student Two offers another suggestion. Student One offers how Silberstein could be used. Megan agrees. Student Five offers more on how Silberstein could be used. Student Two questions/asks for clarification and offers how she sees Britney Spears in the media all the time. This causes the writer to explain more. Megan joins the conversation on Anna Nicole and Britney in the media all the time dealing with substance abuse. Student Five joins in. The writer describes an article she found on Anna and Britney. Megan says they have "very insightful comments on each other's papers" and suggests they incorporate texts from class, "awesome." Notice how the conversation involved much more dynamic uptake with more students *after* Megan openly asked for suggestions from all. I spoke with Megan and Laura afterwards and they both felt that this peer review was a great success.

The *student* questionnaires offered feedback that seems to support Megan's over Laura's view of in-class interactions. Like Laura, one student commented positively on Megan's personality: "I liked the attitude she had. She was always willing to help us. Very dedicated to her job." However, five students commented on what they viewed as Megan's lack of overall participation in the classroom: "She needs to be more obvious in class. Then maybe students will want to go get help. Because it seemed like she wasn't involved." Another said, "As far as having her in the classroom, I did not think it was helpful. I rarely even noticed she was in our classroom. I don't think they need to come to class." Another, "Maybe the tutor could plan some activities and get involved more." Another, "Didn't find it too effective." And the fifth, "She didn't help out that much." Perhaps Megan's initial worry over becoming too much of a TA, and subsequent hesitancy to take on any authoritative instructional role in the classroom (besides peer review leader), actually hindered her from realizing her full potential in the classroom, though it might have helped her during one-to-one tutorials.

Reciprocal Care in Peer Response Writing Groups, and Beyond: Teams Three, Five, and Six

Finding Her "Cool to Care" Niche: Madeleine on Location

The peer review session I was invited to for **Team Three** had a very different feel from the ones I report on with Teams One and Two above. Students in Sydney's class were revising their annotated bibliographies for their final portfolios:

> Ten students are in attendance. Sydney and Madeleine enter the classroom together. Rather than have a peer-review guideline sheet, Sydney simply passes around a handout on annotated bibliographies. Madeleine is sitting in the front row among the students. Sydney gives instructions on where to go from their previous personal responses. They are to partner-up and one, write in pen or highlighter what they can keep for the annotated bibliography, and two, write in what is missing. Information from the longer responses are to be brought down to two-three sentence summaries. Sydney writes these instructions on the board, and says that she and Madeleine will move among the groups. As students begin, Madeleine goes up to Sydney at the front with the assignment sheet and asks for some clarification. Then Madeleine begins to talk with the student next to her about the task. Madeleine uses the instruction sheet to help this student ask questions of her partner's text. Sydney moves quickly from group to group. (Sydney commented during her interview that she felt that Madeleine often lingered too long one-to-one with students

> during such class activities, rather than "roaming the room.") Madeleine refers to an article they read and continues to talk about how that relates to the task. Madeleine then moves to the student's partner, doing the same thing, explaining the task in more detail. Madeleine moves to another student; asks if he's doing ok; repeats the same further explanation. Sydney gathers the class's attention and talks about evaluating the source. As she describes evaluation, she looks over, gesturing to Madeleine. Madeleine adds to what Sydney is saying about evaluation, describing the idea of the credibility of the source and where it came from, or if it might be biased. Then Madeleine continues to move among students. She approaches two young women sitting in the back, and there appears to be some pre-established rapport as they begin to chat and laugh. The students ask about her being sick; they ask about what she studies. (They are off-task, but only for about a minute, and these students are already garrulous before and after Madeleine moves on.) Madeleine leaves the room for two minutes, comes back and sits in her seat. Sydney says pull out another article and do the same process on their own bibliography. Madeleine chats with me a bit. Sydney begins meeting one-to-one with a student up front with his paper. A student close to Madeleine asks what he's supposed to be doing right now. She explains. Then he asks her about a paper. A student behind Madeleine drops a bunch of Altoid mints. She helps him pick them up, and she throws them away. Madeleine spends the rest of the class (about five minutes) writing in her day-planner and reading a paper (maybe hers, maybe a student's?). With five minutes of class-time left, Sydney says they can leave if they're done. Most students begin to leave. Madeleine packs up and leaves as well.

Due to the design of this class activity, I notice that Madeleine seems much more casual and hands-off compared to both Megan (who attended class every day) and Julian. Madeleine also approached students differently. She would somewhat tentatively approach them and ask if they needed any help, rather than just assume they did. In fact, Madeleine's attitude and actions in this peer response facilitation resembled more closely what I saw taking place with the SCSU Team Five below.

Of the ten *student* questionnaires I received back, *all ten* were overwhelmingly positive. Strikingly, while no students made direct reference to the one-to-one tutorials, *nine* students commented in detail on the benefits of having Madeleine in the classroom regularly. Students also wrote much more, and more complexly, than any of the other Teams' student questionnaires. Students talked about the convenience of having a tutor in the know, a tutor closer to the expectations of the class, a tutor they *trusted*. One student wrote: "In English 104 [the first part of the stretch-course] I did struggle in class because I had many questions that I needed to be answered but was scared to ask, but when having a tutor you know that you can ask questions." Another, "The in-class tutor always raised questions in class. She always let us know when we weren't meeting the expectations of the course. For example many of the students were only focusing on content and our tutor told us that we had to focus on meaning." Another, "In-class tutors give the professors a break and also are very helpful to the students when the professor is occupied ... When needing help in class and the teacher was helping another student having her there to answer questions." Another, "We got a lot of attention during class. It was like being one on one." Another, "Not having a tutor [in 104] was somewhat more difficult to receive help because there was only one instructor. Having two has made questions and help a lot faster." Another, "It was weird at first, but later on having the tutor really helped. The in-class tutor was like a TA for the class who goes around and helps a student in need. It really helped me, because the tutor gave me ideas and thoughts to think about what I was writing about." Another, "I had a better understanding because the tutor was willing to be a part of the class." Another, "They help give ideas to the class, as well as brainstorming situations with us." And finally, "She branches out a lot of good ideas during discussion ... I like how she joined class conversations. She always gave her feelings on what an article meant to her. Hearing her thoughts gave me ideas ... Many of my questions were answered because if Sydney was busy the tutor would help me."

Learning Disability and Response-Ability: Gina on Location

Fresh from having taken the same developmental writing course the previous year, Gina from **Team Five** capitalized on the bond she already enjoyed with instructor Mya. During a peer review and response session in week four, I witnessed an amazing moment—something I had never quite seen before—that immediately piqued my interest.

> I noticed one student in particular, Max, having a visibly tough time understanding what he was supposed to be doing, while his two peer group partners seemed to be experienc-

> ing no trouble at all. Gina, who was circulating around the room, later in our interview reported that she saw that Max was having trouble. "I noticed Max looking nervous over in his seat so I went over to see what I could help him with. His partners Kim and Adrianne already had their computers set up and were starting the assignment. Max wasn't as far along. He hadn't even logged into the computer," she said. Gina spent much of the remaining class session helping him get on track with the multiple organizational and communicative tasks students needed to negotiate during this peer review and response session: working with online files, following the response guidelines and instructions, and reading and offering feedback to his group members. Gina told Max not to worry too much about the comments his partners were giving him, but rather to focus on the comments he was writing for them.
>
> As Mya circulated the room she went over to Max's group. Max groggily said "I'm tired today, the weather." Gina continued to good-naturedly and patiently help him navigate the review process. She turned to his two group members at one point for help. Kim came over to help out, succeeded, and then moved back to her computer. At one point, Max deeply sighed and Kim chipped in a tip on commenting. Max said "yeah, yeah, yeah" in relief. A few minutes later, Max said to Gina that he is "falling apart" and "can't concentrate." She continued trying to coach him on how to handle things.
>
> After class, Max came up to me, we said hi, and then he just stood there for a second. I asked how he is doing. He told me that he is not feeling all that well and that he is having a hard time with this peer review. We chatted a little more before he left for his next class.

Later Gina would tell me, "I felt bad for Max because he was very overwhelmed and also not feeling well. I tried to make him feel like he will do much better with his group-mates' advising in a less stressful environment so it's fine that he is not really doing anything during class." Part of the problem, and one that distinguished this class and partnership from others I have studied, was the amount of technology Mya uses in her courses. Mya always teaches in wired, computer-equipped classrooms. So, unlike the peer response sessions I reported on above, the participants in this study not only had to process the typical logistics of peer response, they also had to negotiate the nuances of the technology involved. (Another thing that may have contributed to Max's discomfort, suggested by his approaching me at the end, was my very presence in the classroom to begin with. Perhaps Max's knowing that I was there to observe and potentially report on those observations contributed to the sensory-overload and anxiety he experienced.) The entire visit, I noticed how patient and caring Gina was with Max. And I started to think that there was something very important taking place here.

During a visit one month later, I noticed both Max and his peer response partners taking on much more interactive collaborative roles:

> Max, today, seemed in much better shape—no visible worries, etc. I noticed that rather than frequently asking Gina for help he seemed to be much more involved with his two partners. In contrast to what I witnessed during my earlier visit, Max seemed to have a good grasp of what he was supposed to be doing. He asked his partners a question and they helped him; they asked him questions and he helped them. I was impressed with how these students, especially Kim, were collaborating with Max. In contrast to my last visit, Gina only came over to the group a couple of times. At one point, the group talked about works cited pages and the fact that neither of Max's partners did one, but that he did. Gina ended up spending much more focused time with other students, including a male student who was having difficulty with citations and formatting. Following Nelson's progression, Max seemed to be moving smoothly from dependence to interdependence and independence with his peer response group.

Gina gives her impressions of her involvement with Max and his group members in this second peer review session:

> Like always Max was right on track with what he was supposed to do. He was just double-checking that he was up to speed. I looked at Max's work and realized he was very ahead of the game. He had his e-portfolio set up very nicely. He already had one paper posted and was almost ready to post another. He then asked me to look over the second paper he was going to post before he posted it. I looked at what he changed and what Mya asked him to look over. He took everything Mya said and changed it. His paper looked very nice. I told him it looked great and it should be ready to post.

> He wanted a second opinion so Mya was called over. I was very happy that Max feels so comfortable to ask my opinion. I have noticed that every class he calls me over at least once. I am happy to talk with him and assure him he is on track with everything.

In their end-of-term questionnaires, ten out of eleven *students* felt Gina's presence in class was beneficial, and only one was ambivalent. (The ambivalent student only wrote a couple of yes's or no's indeterminately.) Several students commented on their overall impressions of having an in-class tutor: "makes help only a nod away. It was great." Another, "She was very helpful with papers and assignments. I think it was a good idea to have one in every class." And, harking back to the comments by students involved with Julian and Anne's overall unsuccessful partnership in Team One who felt that their course-based tutor did not know what was going on in the course, one student wrote: "I liked it because it gave you someone to help you with your work that actually sits in the class and knows what's going on ... so maybe people feel more comfortable that way." I also took the chance to interview the student Gina and Kim worked so closely with, Max. He told me that he really appreciated the attention he received from Gina, his group members, and Mya. He said he especially appreciated Kim's help (for more on this case study, especially Gina's and Max's personal stories, see Corbett "Learning").

Paying Care and Trust Forward: Kim and Penny on Location

As mentioned above, two of the students from Team Five's class, Kim and Penny, were recruited to become course-based tutors for the following semester with an experienced adjunct instructor, Jake. **Team Six**, illustrates what can happen if continuity is carried forward (genealogically, if you will) from student-to-tutor, from tutor-to-tutor, from instructor-to-instructor, from tutor-to-instructor. One of the several threads that linked the participants from the two courses was the interaction between Kim and Max. Recall, Max and Kim were peer response group partners and, like Sara, Kim found the experience of working with Max highly rewarding. While it would be easy to overestimate the effect Max had on Kim's performance as either a student writer with Mya or as a course-based tutor the subsequent term with Jake, one cannot help but believe there was indeed some inspirational paying forward. As with the other case-study teams, I sat in on and took field notes of in-class peer response sessions with this team. The sessions I witnessed fell very much on a continuum of directive/controlling and nondirective/facilitative interaction witnessed especially with Madeleine from

Team Three and Gina from Team Five. In short, in the sessions I witnessed, Kim acted much the way Sydney from Team Three reported Madeleine acting during class discussions—more outgoing and authoritative—and Penny acted a bit more like Megan from Team Two—more reserved during class discussions, but more hands-on during peer response sessions. When Jake started addressing the entire class for the session with Kim, Kim joined in with Jake very much as a co-teacher, even finishing his sentences a couple of times. In contrast, when Jake spoke to the entire class that Penny was attached to, she did not join in like Kim had. However, once students became engaged in responding to each other's essays, both Kim and Penny became very involved in the groups. Jake had encouraged both classes to write on each other's essays as well as talk about them. Both Kim and Penny did not hesitate to join in on writing comments down on student papers as they discussed their suggestions. But these tutors went even further in embracing authoritative roles in their respective courses, and together.

During my interviews with all participants in Team Six, and from the journals both Kim and Penny were keeping on a class-by-class basis, I came upon some compelling findings. Due to the fact that Kim and Penny were both working with the same instructor, Jake, albeit in two different courses, this team had the opportunity to collaborate much more interactively than any other CBT partnership I've studied. And they took full advantage of that opportunity. Allow me to end the reporting on the case studies and stories in this book by quoting at length from Penny and Kim's journals. (One of the strengths of both Nelson's and Brooke, Mirtz, and Evans's studies are the extensive amount of reporting and analyses the authors provide from participant journals.) We will begin with excerpts from Penny's journal:

> **Tuesday, April 13th**
>
> Yesterday, Jake handed out the assignment that Kim and I came up with. The assignment is much more specific so the students are able to understand and follow it. The assignment is called "The American Dream Museum Exhibit" [See Appendix D]. The students are to get in groups and bring any kind of artifact that they think represents the American Dream. On Thursday, the students will bring at least ten artifacts to class and explain to their group why they chose that. On Thursday, students will also narrow down their items to five each. These five will be the items they include in their exhibit and presentation. In a few weeks, the groups will present their museum of what they think represents the American Dream.

Thursday, April 15th

Today, the groups met with artifacts they brought in or images they printed and cut out. I sat with group one for a while, just observing and listening to what they had to say about what they brought in. It was interesting to see the different perspectives they had of the American Dream. Each member brought something different, but in the same way, that one artifact connected with a group member's different artifact. One group member printed out a picture of a white picket fence, and another member brought a picture from the newspaper of a perfect-looking house. I suggested that the members can use both of those images in the presentation to add to the exhibit.

One member brought all portable items of technology (cell phone, iPod, etc.) and another member brought a McDonald's to-go bag. Both members had the different explanations for the artifacts, but I pointed out one way in which they tied together. I mentioned that both could represent mobility and how valuable time is to Americans. As I came back to this group later in the class, they had built off that idea even more.

As I moved onto other groups, and listened to what they had to say about their items, I was impressed with how different the results were. After listening to each member give me an explanation of all the artifacts they brought, I told them about things that I had not heard from the other groups, but I heard from them. Since they are covering the same topic, it's important that they all have different artifacts so things don't get repetitive when they present their exhibits.

Wednesday, April 28th

Jake sent the following email:

Hi Kim and Penny,

I wanted to give you both a heads up that I will not be in class on Thursday. However I do not want to cancel class since each group needs to work on their exhibit design and layout.

While I do not expect them to stay for the entire class, I would hope that they take the opportunity to organize their exhibit in detail and have each member give a tour of their artifacts and introductions. Each of you can provide your feedback and insights to the groups.

If either of you have any questions, please feel free to email me or call or text my cell.

Thanks and I'll see you on Tuesday.

Jake

Thursday, April 29th

As the students walked into class, I explained to them what the agenda would be. They knew Jake wasn't going to be in class, so I told them once I met with their groups, they were free to leave class. Each group had to explain what their title of their exhibit was, read their introductions, and give me a tour of what each artifact in their exhibit was. After each group was done presenting to me, I asked questions to keep them thinking. If they had artifacts they didn't explain well, I asked them what the artifact's symbolism or representation was of the American Dream. Each group was well-organized and knew how they were going to present the exhibit to the class. I made sure to ask the students how and where in the classroom were they going to set up all of their artifacts. If I was unsure of a question, I sent Jake a text. I did not want to tell the students the wrong answer, because it was Jake who was grading the presentations, not me. Before the groups left, I told them to come to class on time the following Tuesday and to be ready to present. Next Tuesday and Thursday the groups will be presenting their exhibits.

The following excerpts are taken from Kim's journal entries. The first one offers her take on the day Jake was not in class. The latter two provide reporting on the days students delivered their "American Dream Museum" exhibits near the end of the term.

4/29/2010

Today was very cool. Prof J. was unable to attend class. So I got to act as the prof for the day ☺ The students went over their exhibits and what they have so far. They both seemed to be very good and well thought out so far. However, only two people from the second group were in class today so I didn't really get a great sense of how their exhibit will go. Both groups read their introductions as if they were presenting it to the class ... What I enjoyed most was that even though these introductions were not being peer reviewed the students gave each other criticism and helped them reword things as well as encouraged them when they enjoyed what their peer wrote!

5/4/2010

TODAY'S THE BIG DAY!! ☺ The students have been working on their exhibits and they will finally be able to present them. Unfortunately, one student was absent. Thus, one of the groups was short. Also two students came late so they were unable to present their projects today with their groups ☹ The projects included a movie (*The Pursuit of Happiness*), a baseball card, lots of pictures, poems and songs, a water bottle, and more. I loved the explanations and after their intros last class and then again today, I could see a huge difference. The students who actually came today had made the changes to their intros for the objects and they came out very well ... The students really went in depth and took the explanation to another level. Also, the students didn't really seem nervous. They knew why they chose their five objects and discussed them well. One of the poems that was shared also made me think a lot. It was titled "The American Dream" and the student used the poem to stress how the American dream is represented in a negative way. The poem basically goes into how once people are living the so called "American Dream," making money and doing well for themselves, they forget about the individuals who do not have wealth or even places to rest their head at night ☹

5/6/2010

> This semester is coming to an end ☹ We started the class off by having the last three students present their projects. These three students actually presented their projects separately because their groups went on Tuesday. It really made me remember back to the second and third class hearing the students read their essays and being embarrassed and rushing through them, whereas today they mostly spoke clearly and with confidence. I could definitely see the growth in such a short amount of time.

In their questionnaires, *students* from both of Team Six's courses reported very much the same sort of high satisfaction with the courses as with Team Five above.

DISCUSSION: DIRECTION, NONDIRECTION, AND MISDIRECTION IN THE CBT CLASSROOM

The above scenarios begin to clearly illustrate just how complicated—or complimentary—things can get when you combine various instructional aspects of the parent genres, as well as different participant personalities, goals, and instructional experiences and backgrounds. Of all the teams, **Team One** I initially thought would be the most successful. Julian, with all his experience, seemed like the ideal "writing advisor" tutor for this project. Anne, likewise had the experience, was studying in the field of Composition and Rhetoric, and showed early enthusiasm toward the project in general. Yet Julian summarized the overall experience as going "sort of poorly, less than mediocre." Julian pointed to two primary reasons he felt the partnership did not work well: lack of communication with Anne, and confusion as to what his specific role was in the class. Julian felt that his minimal presence in the classroom affected his relationship with the class, creating an awkward, "ambivalent space" between himself and the students. He felt that the students and he never got to know each other. So, he said, students were "like 'Julian's going to be our writing consultant, is going to be part of the class,' and then I show up twice and nobody ever hears from me." Anne voiced two main reasons why she felt the partnership floundered: her lack of collaboration with Julian, and Julian's nondirective instructional approach. On her initial high-hopes that quickly began to fall, she said: "When I met Julian at the beginning I thought this would be great; this has such great potential because we both have such similar philosophies, basically teaching philosophy ... But [laughter] in practice it wasn't quite as good."

Despite the relatively greater amount of tutoring experience both Julian and Anne possessed, they were ironically unable to perform with the sort of flexibility and adaptability that the other teams displayed. While we might point to instances where Julian did get directive, as when he more or less "forced" the student to read his paper aloud during the second peer review, I would argue that Julian did not really do that bad a job during the peer reviews, evidenced by him trying to play what he felt was his role of question-posing facilitator, or "reserved advisor"—in short, to play the role of Decker's "meta-tutor, encouraging students to tutor each other" ("Diplomatic" 27). The greatest tension seemed to be in Julian's debatably inflexible minimalist/nondirective approach. Repeatedly, as illustrated especially in the peer reviews above, the data point to instances where Julian was trying perhaps too hard to play it safe, to attempt at all costs to meet what he felt were Anne's expectations, to stick to the prompts closely and carefully during interactions with students. Perhaps, as with Megan, Julian worried too much about taking on a teacherly role. His feeling that Anne was the teacher, and he was there to be a "reserved advisor," may have actually confounded the students' expectations that he should offer whatever direct suggestions he could. His attempt to be as peer-like as possible may have had the opposite effect. Clark's study of directive/nondirective tutoring with students who labeled themselves "poor" writers, found that these students perceived their tutors as more successful when the tutors were directive, contributing "many ideas" ("Perspectives" 41). In contrast to the case studies of Teams Three, Five, and Six where tutors embraced their roles as authority figures, Julian's attempt to stick to what he felt were Anne's expectations, coupled with his limited presence in the classroom, only bewildered students who, it seems, wanted to know more than anything what *he* thought. Julian's repeated efforts to stay within Anne's expectations came across to student's as unwillingness to model a sense of "what would you do?" Further, while I've been tempted to make tentative claims about Julian's actions during tutorials in terms of gender roles, like Black, Denny, and Judith Butler I believe gender is performative based on context. Black argues that though feminist theorists have frequently claimed that talk between women is "cooperative, supportive, non-competitive, nurturing, and recursive" her extensive study of teacher-to-student conferences revealed that

> female teachers dominate female students just as male teachers do ... they are less likely to cooperatively overlap their speech ... female students initiate fewer revision strategies to female teachers and hear less praise from female teachers ... All this together does not add up to the picture of cooperation, support, and shared control that is often presented as characteris-

> tic of female-to-female speech. (68; also see Denny 101-02)

While we saw the same sorts of instructional and conversational "domination" during the one-to-one tutorials from Madeleine, Megan, as well as Julian, a host of other contextual forces worked to undermine the success of Team One.

For **Team Two,** overall, Laura and Megan reported enjoying working together very much. Megan talked about initial role negotiations with Laura:

> It was kind of hard because I'm not a student and I'm not her teaching assistant. But I'm not involved in the grading, but I'm supposed to help them ... it was an opportunity for the students to get some of the most personal and helpful advice in their writing, because they have someone who's there who's not intimidating, because it's not their professor ... I think at the beginning she was thinking that one day I could lead the class. And so I wasn't sure [laughter] what to do.

Megan explained that she worried she would become "more of the TA or assistant TA and not the tutor." As we noted earlier, she was relieved when other, less authoritative roles were agreed upon.

Laura commented on how pleasant Megan's personality was, how she was always smiling and cheerful, how she always had a positive attitude, and how she was easy to talk to and work with. In contrast to Megan's sentiments above, Laura described her working relationship with Megan in terms of wanting to keep their interactions as peer-like as possible: "I kind of see her as my peer. Instead of asking her to do this and that I wanted to get her feedback. We kind of designed the class together." Laura described how early in the quarter she and Megan would meet once a week to discuss weekly schedules, class plans, and upcoming assignments. They would also have "meta-teaching" conversations after class. Laura described Megan's role as "conversation partner" who would "have a lot of things to say about texts" during conversations in class (though she did not distinguish between whole-class conversations and conversations involving peer response).

However, we saw that Megan and Laura had different perceptions of Megan's usefulness in the classroom. While Laura felt that Megan was an important day-to-day in-class player, Megan *and* the students felt that she wasn't quite living up to her participative potential. And while I think she did a great job as "peer review person," especially in the second sessions, students didn't seem to get the same sense of the importance of her presence. Perhaps the introduction of the "oral" peer review confused the students at first and it took a little bit of getting used to before they could feel the full benefits of that method. In the fourth edition of *A Short Course in Writing*, Bruffee distinguishes between two forms of peer review. According to Bruffee, *corresponding* is a more exacting and rigorous form where students write to each other about their papers, and *conferring* is an immediately responsive, conversational form more attuned to the writer's needs. Bruffee argues that "the most helpful kind of constructive conversation combines the two ... So in peer review you write to each other about your essays first, and then you talk about them" (170; also see Gere and Stevens). It seems that, by the end, Team Two was certainly moving in this two-fold feedback direction, exercising and flexing students' abilities to negotiate directive and nondirective strategies, and Megan's ability to coach these peer-to-peer pedagogical skills. It also seems that from the first to the second peer response session, students were moving from dependence to interdependence. Concurrently, it appears that Megan and Laura were moving away from directiveness and more toward a more minimalist facilitative role. This supports Nelson's claims regarding the inverse relationship between students taking and tutors/instructors relinquishing control when working toward successful peer response. Simply put, by that second peer response session I witnessed, the attitude, action, and language of control and directiveness had shifted from Megan to the students. This also coincides with Harris's four reasons why writers need writing tutors, that valuable analytic link between tutoring one-to-one and in small groups. While control seemed to flow from Megan to the students explicitly realizing Harris's first reason—encouraging student independence in collaborative talk—it might have more implicitly helped students realize the other three reasons: assisting students with metacognitive acquisition of strategic knowledge; assisting with knowledge of how to interpret, translate, and apply assignments and teacher comments; and assisting with affective concerns. Yet, overall, students still wanted more from Megan in the classroom.

Madeleine and Sydney from **Team Three** expressed mixed reviews of their partnership. The tutor, Madeleine, narrated her satisfaction with the experience from start to finish. She enjoyed all aspects of her involvement: working with Sydney; working with students; and working with the subject of the course, race and citizenship in the nation. On her initial interactions with students, Madeleine said:

> I think at first they were like, "What the heck, who is this person?" They weren't mad or anything [laughter]. They were just kind of like "ok." They didn't know why I was there, but it was cool. After a while they just thought of me as kind of like another student ... They really seemed to appreciate the things that I said in class and after a while I think it was really

> comfortable ... And they didn't feel, at least as far as I know, they didn't feel like I was trying to be authoritative.

And on her initial role negotiations with Sydney, Madeleine reported: "At first I didn't know what my job would be in the class. And we were just like trying to work it out the first couple of weeks of the quarter." Madeleine goes on to describe how she soon found her niche in the classroom as "discussion participant." During an early class discussion of readings, Madeleine joined in. Afterwards, Sydney praised Madeleine, telling her that she felt the students had participated in a way they "might not have been able to and she [Sydney] might not have been able to. She felt like the students listen to me. Not really more than they listen to her, but they tend to agree with her. So whatever she's saying, whatever she's contributing to the discussion, they think 'oh that's the right way.'"

Sydney's take on the partnership, however, portrays a much more conflicted point of view. Sydney said that she was initially worried that someone else's presence in the classroom would make her feel like she was being watched, but that, fortunately, did not end up being the case. This may be due to her impressions that, echoing Madeleine's own comments, Madeleine really took on more of a peer role in the classroom, seeming much like just another student. Sydney did, however, detail further initial misgivings that—in her mind—ended up affecting the rest of the quarter:

> Initially there was a lot of frustration just trying to match two personalities, two kinds of teaching styles, trying to negotiate where roles were ... I remember the first couple of days I felt like there was a little bit of showing off going on on her part. Maybe she felt the need to prove herself to show [herself] as capable as the TA. Maybe she was trying to show me; I don't know. And I felt that that kind of shut down conversations with my students a little bit because they might have felt intimidated a little bit you know.

But Sydney also talked about how she eventually came to view her interactions with Madeleine in a different light: "In the end I think it took us a while, but I feel like in the end we finally at least began to kind of click and mesh." A big part of this eventually-realized mutual understanding may have something to do with Madeleine's overall motives for and attitude toward this course. In her own words: "The most important thing for me to teach the students was to be active learners in the classroom. I hoped that they would view my enthusiasm for the content as an example of it actually being cool to care." I believe it was this ultimate clicking and meshing that I observed late in the term.

While we might rightly question Madeleine's performance during one-to-one tutorials, I certainly maintain my belief that Madeleine's authoritative style was effective and valuable in the classroom. Delpit makes a related point that hints at a possible reason why the diverse students from Team Three identified so closely with Madeleine:

> The "man (person) of words," be he or she preacher, poet, philosopher, huckster, or rap song creator, receives the highest form of respect in the black community. The verbal adroitness, the cogent and quick wit, the brilliant use of metaphorical language, the facility in rhythm and rhyme, evident in the language of preacher Martin Luther King, Jr., boxer Muhammad Ali, comedienne Whoppi Goldberg, rapper L.L. Cool J., and singer and songwriter Billie Holiday, and many inner-city black students, *may all be drawn upon to facilitate school learning*. (*Other* 57; emphasis added)

Another way to consider the implications of Madeleine's performance is when moving tutors to classrooms we could encourage a more authoritative approach, but when they move back to the center (or wherever else one-to-one or small-group tutorials happen) tutors should resist the temptation to overuse what they know about the course and the instructor's expectations. One of the reasons the tutorials conducted by Madeleine, and to large extent with Megan and Julian (Appendix C), seemed so tutor-centric was because all three of these tutors tried perhaps much too hard to speculate on what the teacher wanted. Most of the linguistic feature and cue ratios—total words spoken, references to the TA or assignment prompts, and interruptions versus main channel overlaps and joint productions—detail salient imbalances, imbalances that overwhelmingly point to almost complete tutor control. While this discursive imbalance luckily did not seem to affect the overall successful partnerships of Teams Two and Three, it certainly did not help the unsuccessful collaboration in Team One. The overarching lesson? Tutors might hold on a little tighter to some nondirective methods and moves that could place agency back in the hands and minds of the students. Of course, unlike the other tutors, Madeleine had not been exposed to the literature on directive/nondirective tutoring, nor could I find any indication that she was encouraged to practice a particularly nondirective method. Perhaps, if she had received a bit of training in directive/nondirective strategies, then Madeleine's fight-for-the-floor session might have sounded more like Sam's parallel session, or even more like the sort of non-intrusive, flexible collaboration I witnessed during my visit to Madeleine and Sydney's classroom during peer response. Maybe then Madeleine could have exhibited some of those nondirective methods and moves showcased by Sam from Team Four in all of her one-to-one tutorials. Yet perhaps, as Nelson discovered, Madeleine had earlier moments of directiveness, but as the course moved on, and by the time I saw her more "laid-back" attitude and action in the classroom near the end of the term, she had pulled back on her interventions as students became more self-directed, interdependent, and to varying degrees independent.

The tutor for **Team Five**, Gina, felt her involvement as a course-based tutor for the class went "different, but better than I thought it would be." She thought it was wonderful that students had the option of asking either her or Mya questions during classroom activities. She also felt she was able to engage with students on a personal as well as academic level, even though she said that she usually sat at the head of the class with Mya when she was not circulating around the room. She also did all of the readings for the course, but only did one writing assignment to show students how she approached it. (Something none of the other case-study tutors undertook.) Gina said that if she could give other course-based tutors any advice, it would be not to overly worry or hesitate to approach and interact with students. She felt that in the first few weeks she did not want to bother or interfere too much, but then she started to realize that students really appreciated her interventionist attention.

The instructor, Mya, said that she and Gina's familiarity allowed Gina to take a very active and highly informed role in assistant teaching for the course. She said Gina started off a little slow at first, but very soon she felt that students started to warm up to her and really lean on her for questions and support. She (echoing Madeleine from Team Three) would often help jump-start class discussions if students were initially silent. She felt that Gina was like a "life preserver" that she could throw out at any time in the classroom for any particular student who needed it. Although, she did feel this class was stronger than usual in terms of their engagement, she very much appreciated having Gina close by to help circulate and give more individual attention to others. She said that even though Gina did not say a lot in class all the time, she was very upbeat and always had wonderfully positive energy (reminiscent of Megan from Team Two). Mya said she believes Gina's LD actually enabled her to make even stronger connections with other students, especially Max, though she said "you can't tell Gina has a LD by just talking with her." Mya praised Gina's communication and organization skills. When I asked her if she would do anything differently next time, Mya said that she would have liked to plan things out a little more with Gina, perhaps regular weekly meetings, so Gina had more say in what was going on (I have heard this advice several times before with participants in CBT). When I asked her if she'd be willing to have another tutor attached to her class, she said, laughing, "I would not want to do it without one." She felt that having a tutor did not demand any extra time on her part and was only a benefit. She felt that working with Gina made her think just how important it is to slow down sometimes and make sure things are clear to all students.

Much like the in-class peer response session I witnessed with Madeleine and Sydney from Team Three, I saw Gina responding at the point of need of the students. In other words, *the potential for the tutor to control or over-direct in this situation was mitigated due to the fact that the students themselves initiated, and to a large degree controlled, the call for tutorial assistance.* Yet scholars disagree on what might be the best setting for fostering such student-centered control, including minority students and students with LDs. In "Cultural Diversity in the Writing Center" Judith Kilborn describes these contrasting philosophies in terms of those who believe either: one, minority and diverse students should be mainstreamed into the general population "to prepare them to interact with the diverse population they will meet in the workplace"; or two, "minority students are best served by services designed and run by minorities for minorities; they feel that such services provide a sense of community and cultural pride" (393). In "Discourses of Disability and Basic Writing" Amy Vidali questions a claim made by Barber-Fendley and Hamel that LD students should be separated out from the writing classroom, especially the basic writing classroom, for additional support. Vidali argues, rather, that similarities abound between LD and non-LD basic writing students: they are both talked about in terms of difficulty and overcoming deficits, they often share identities and classrooms, and both are "defined according to a dominant (white, male, abled) other" (53). Vidali urges us to do what we can to unify basic writing and LD pedagogy. She believes that LD students would then benefit from the same structural support systems afforded basic writers in all their various diversities. I find myself agreeing with Vidali. When we consider the effects of the interactions of both Gina and Kim with Max, Vidali's assertions begin to make very good sense—for all participants. In a way, then, the arguments for more unified instructional support systems for diverse students echo the arguments for closer writing classroom and peer tutoring coordination described in the Introduction (see Corbett "Learning" for more on this particular case study).

All participants from **Team Six** voiced high satisfaction with their experiences together. Overall, Kim described her experiences as highly positive and rewarding: "I felt that working with the students taught me a lot. It actually helped me with my own study habits and certainly helped me become more patient." Reflecting back on their interactions, like Sara, Kim found the experience of working with Max rewarding. She told me that she would sometimes email Max when she had questions about an assignment. She went on to say:

> When working with Max I remember him being a very intelligent young man. He had wonderful thoughts and ideas and always put one hundred percent into all of his work. Even when doing public speaking projects Max gave his all. He was frightened to speak in front of the class but, as his partner, I saw him practice over and over until he was confident. Sometimes Max just needed someone there to repeat or explain the assignments as well as a partner who was willing to practice with him over and over until he felt comfortable.

Likewise, the other tutor, Penny, reported an overall positive experience, especially in relation to her field of study, Elementary Education:

> It helped me jump into being a mentor or teacher of some sort. It helped encourage me to dive right in and help students, no matter what age. Working with college age students for this project was a new experience, but still had the same concept of teaching and helping students. I had to figure out the correct way to communicate with them and how to approach them. I learned a lot from the experience, mostly about myself and how capable I was to help others.

The instructor, Jake, during our interview talked at length about the project, highlighting how much he felt all participants benefited from their close collaboration. He said, "the key to all of this, in my mind, both for the tutors and me the instructor, is flexibility and being open to different approaches and different ways of structuring the class." He said that he thinks it is important not just to find out how the instructor wants to realize participant roles, but to also consider the peer tutors' desires. (He did express some relief, however, when he saw just how active and involved, typically shy and quiet, Penny was during small-group work, compared to her more ostensibly passive performances during whole-class discussions.) On the benefits of having developmental students who themselves had just taken the course as peer tutors he said: "It let students know that here is someone who went through the same struggles as you went through and were successful in their journey through the course." He went on to say that he felt that course-based tutors do not even need to be A students to have a positive effect. He feels there is some benefit in being able to say "Look these are real people who worked real hard to work through the writing process to improve their writing, and they are just here to help." Jake said that he also gained quite a bit from this experience. He felt that the American Dream project, especially, made him consider the possibilities for students designing their own group projects.

He felt that the creativity and care Kim and Penny demonstrated throughout that project, in their negotiations of what pedagogically might work, "might encourage me to be more creative. They [the tutors] have the benefit of tapping into many different professors who are equally or more creative than I am, and I have no problem stealing from them and learning from them."

What I believe I saw emerge with Team Six was a heightened level of collaborative trust among the participants. This heightened level of trust enabled Kim and Penny to take active interventions in all phases of the students' writing processes—from invention, to revision, to delivery. In "A Non-Coda," Muriel Harris revisits her 1992, "Collaboration Is Not Collaboration Is Not Collaboration," where she delineated the boundaries between one-to-one tutoring and peer response. In her more recent essay, she argues that peer response groups could be utilized for pre-writing activities like brainstorming how to approach the assignment, trading ideas on how to incorporate readings, and initial thoughts on topics and the narrowing of topics—if instructors are willing and able to facilitate such activities. This is precisely the sort of generative pre-writing activities we saw facilitated with such aplomb by Kim and Penny in the "American Dream" project. While the experienced tutors from the UW case studies were worried about trying to make sure students were meeting the expectations of the instructor's assignments, these "novice" tutors were creating their own assignments and doing all they could to assist students in generative inquiry, and all other phases, in order to succeed and learn something. In short, and even more than Madeleine, these tutors were vividly enacting and modeling creative and critical thought and action for the benefit of their peers/mentees—something all teachers of writing hope and strive to do.

My research over the years, including these portraits of CBT teachers, students, and tutors in action, has persuaded me that the pros of encouraging tutors to practice at the edge of their expertise, by-and-large, outweigh the cons. Case studies like the kind presented here could help all stakeholders in peer-to-peer teaching and learning consider strategies and rationales for what methods might be characterized as directive or nondirective in various circumstances and how to try to resist moving too far along the continuum in either direction, in a variety of situations, in and out of the classroom. Perhaps with the knowledge gained regarding directive and nondirective pedagogical strategies and methods, CBT practitioners can continue encouraging colleagues (and their students and tutors) in writing classrooms and in writing centers to make and map similar explorations—to take similar complimentary journeys—serving center *and* classroom.

CHAPTER FIVE

CONCLUSION: TOWARD TEACHER/ STUDENT, CLASSROOM/CENTER HYBRID CHOICES

> Placing students and tutors at the center of classroom practice, on-location tutoring reforms classroom hierarchical relations and institutional structures; it shows students (tutors and the students with whom they work) that their work as knowledge makers matters and that they have much to contribute to one another, to faculty, and to the institution as a whole.
>
> – Laurie Grobman and Candace Spigelman

> The line it is drawn
> The curse it is cast
> The slow one now
> Will later be fast
> As the present now
> Will later be past
> The order is
> Rapidly fadin'
> And the first one now
> Will later be last
> For the times they are a-changin'
>
> – Bob Dylan

In the Introduction and Chapter One I discussed several variables that come into play as a result of the melding of the various parent instructional genres that inform the work of CBT. I explored the genealogy of CBT, theoretically locating it within the context of the classroom/center collaborative debate. I moved on to describe a taxonomy of the major parent genres that intermingle and hybridize in CBT—writing center tutoring, writing fellows programs, peer writing groups, and supplemental instruction—to offer participants an array of instructional choices and considerations that can at times confuse or overwhelm, and at other times liberate and substantially supplement classroom and one-to-one teaching and tutoring. I then lingered in detail on the critical issues of authority, role and trust negotiation via the directive/nondirective tutoring continuum, placing special emphasis on reasons tutors may need to renegotiate the typical hands-off, nondirective one-to-one philosophy when negotiating the "play of differences" between one-to-one and one-to-more instructional situations.

I'd like to begin my concluding thoughts by returning to two questions—in relation to the directive/nondirective instructional continuum—I asked in the Introduction: What are teachers, tutors, and student writers getting out of these experiences, and what effects do these interactions have on participant instructional choices and identity formations as teachers and learners? And how soon should developing/developmental student writers, potential writing tutors, and classroom instructors or teaching assistants get involved in the authoritative, socially and personally complex acts of collaborative peer-to-peer teaching and learning? I'll begin by framing my tentative answers to these questions in terms of how the interrelated pedagogical concepts of authority/trust building and directive/nondirective instructional negotiations played out in all teams. I'll move on to offer some implications of the studies and stories presented in this book for one-to-one and small-group tutorials, peer review and response, and the various choices program leaders can consider in building, strengthening, or experimenting with CBT.

DIRECTIVE/NONDIRECTIVE TUTORING: IMPLICATIONS FOR TUTORING ONE-TO-ONE AND IN THE CLASSROOM

The true value of CBT, and the lessons learned from experiments in pushing the limits of pedagogical peer authority and expertise, lies in the choices it offers teachers, tutors, student writers, and program leaders and the implications these choices have on the places we work and the people we work with. When participants were brought into the closer instructional orbits afforded by CBT, the biggest adjustments they described as having to make involved negotiations of instructional authority and roles, which also brought up the gravity of mutual trust(worthiness). Megan, the tutor from Team Two, worried about being too teacherly. She expressed relief when she and Laura agreed on less-authoritative roles for her in the classroom. But, as the interview and questionnaire data illustrate, both Megan and the students ended up feeling that Megan did not meet her full potential as an in-class tutor. Bruffee's double-bind we spoke of in the Introduction was plainly elucidated in Megan's conflicted desire to be both a peer—to appear just like one of the students and to be subsequently approachable—and to offer as much help and support to these students as possible. In a sense, the TA Laura trusted in Megan's abilities as an experienced writing center tutor to be able to balance directive/nondirective and teacherly/studently roles in the classroom; but Megan perhaps did not trust herself enough to lean a little more toward an authoritative role in the classroom, *even when offered and encouraged to act-out this role by Laura.* As the literature on CBT practice points to repeatedly, tutors put in closer contact with the expectations of the writing instructors with whom they are paired will have a difficult time negotiating their tutoring approach—often times swinging too far toward the extreme ends of the directive/nondirective instructional continuum. And as Laura described, even though she and Megan did a lot of planning of the course together, students did not seem to know that Megan was that involved with the design of the course. Perhaps if she had embraced her role as a co-designer of the course a bit more vocally, taken ownership of the course like the tutors from Team Six, students would have viewed her as, in fact, much more integral to their learning for the course.

Yet, I must qualify these statements regarding Megan's engagement with in-class activities, and the course as a whole, as she did take an active role in peer review. One interesting consideration for future peer review facilitation efforts is the idea of the "meta-tutor" (Decker). Recall Julian trying to live up to what he felt was his role as "reserved advisor," a tutor who does not try to necessarily give suggestions directly to student papers, but rather tries to provide suggestions to students on how to tutor each other. This idea becomes problematic in light of the directive/nondirective continuum. If tutors are trying to be good meta-tutors, and, like Julian, speaking too much about revising in the abstract, then they may only confuse students. I do not think there is anything wrong—indeed it might be better in many cases—if the peer review facilitator is willing to play a role closer to just another student reviewer. Then students in that particular response group would gain the benefits of direct modeling of things to comment on. Encouraging the use of a mix of direct suggestions along with the sorts of open-ended questioning and prompting that lead other members of the response group to contribute, might be a better way to think about preparing tutors for peer response facilitation. By the second session I believe Megan had realized a great mix—one that allowed for substantial *conversational momentum* between students—encouraging students to rapidly and energetically uptake each other's responses and suggestions.

Madeleine from Team Three felt she was authoritative but not authoritarian—an important distinction—in the classroom. Madeleine referred to herself as a "discussion participant" in the classroom. But she, the instructor Sydney, and the students clearly intimated that Madeleine was really much more like a discussion leader. Sydney described how her initial misgivings about Madeleine began to transform as she came to realize that what she initially perceived as Madeleine's weakness actually ended up being her strength—Madeleine's willingness to act as a conversation leader, even antagonist, during class discussions. Paulo Freire believed this was an important, and often overlooked, aspect of teaching. In his last book *Pedagogy of Freedom*, Freire urged

> It is not only of interest to students but extremely important to students to perceive the differences that exist among teachers over the comprehension, interpretation, and appreciation, sometimes widely differing, of problems and questions that arise in the day-to-day learning situations of the classroom. (24)

I linked Madeleine's instructional style to patterns of AAVE communication in Chapter Three. It may have been a combination of Madeleine's more natural AAVE communicative patterns, coupled with her passion for both the topic of the course and her desire to help these students do well in the course, that all contributed to her performances in the class. Mutual participant trust was a key factor in this partnership. Madeleine's willingness to take an active co-teaching role in the classroom added to the trust she earned from the students she interacted with on a day-to-day basis, and to the eventual trust (albeit qualified) she earned from Sydney. Yet, for all my conflicted feelings regarding Madeleine's highly directive style—whether or not her directives were a "good" thing—I cannot help but wish that she could have played a slightly less directive role during her one-to-ones. Especially as evidenced in that long session with the student who kept trying to voice her ideas and opinions, with all the attending overlaps and even heightened emotion involved, I wish that Madeleine could have balanced her passion for moving students toward more feasible interpretations of the text with more traditionally nondirective approaches demanding increased listening and open-ended questioning.

Going back to Harris's four categories—exploratory talk, acquisition of strategic knowledge, negotiation of assignment prompts and teacher comments, and affective concerns—we saw Sam helping students with aspects of all four. Harris's categories are important and can be linked to—and offer pedagogical answers to—other categorical conceptions of educational and professional learning and development. Chris Thaiss and Terry Zawacki, for example, posit that undergraduate students' conceptions of academic writing involve a complicated matrix of variables that include generalized standards of academic writing, disciplinary conventions, sub-disciplinary conventions, institutional and departmental cultures and policies, and personal goals and idiosyncratic likes and dislikes (from both student writers and their instructors). In their four-year study of teachers and students engaged in writing across the disciplines at George Mason University, the authors argue that as students move through their undergraduate educations, negotiating these variables, they experience roughly three developmental stages: in the first stage they use their limited academic experience to construct a general view of academic writing as "what the teachers expect;" in the second stage, after encountering a number of different teacher expectations, students develop a sense of idiosyncrasy or "they all want different things;" and in the third stage, which not all students reach, "a sense of coherence-within-diversity, understanding expectations as a rich mix of many ingredients" (139).

Sam emerged as what I have come to believe as one of the most sophisticated and methodologically sound of any tutor I've witnessed during one-to-one tutorials, moving students perhaps at least toward Thaiss and Zawacki's second stage. But she may even be helping developmental students, well in advance of disciplinary courses, toward awareness of the third stage. The authors claim that the data from the instructors and students they studied point to the notion that third-stage students experience a mix of personal goals with disciplinary expectations. Of all the tutors, Sam encouraged the most exploratory talk with students—students generally spoke much more and were much more invested in the one-to-one tutorials. As Megan finally realized in facilitating peer response groups, Sam realized tremendous conversational momentum with students. Sam helped nudge students toward acquisition of strategic knowledge by focusing primarily on the big picture with each student's paper: she usually spent much time talking—and getting students to talk about—their claim. She spent considerable time talking (and listening) about structural issues like topic sentences and how they should relate to the claim. Her ability not to get too caught up with the assignment prompts or teacher comments actually seemed to work in her favor; she appeared focused on the writing and the writer she was working with rather than worry unnecessarily about the prompt. All of these moves took into account both the students' purposes and Sam's knowledge of academic discourse from the disciplines of Biology and English. And, more implicitly I would argue, Sam tended to students' affective needs largely by just listening carefully to their concerns, allowing plenty of time for them to think through ideas. From my experience, she provides a fine model of the sorts of moves all tutors and teachers can consider: careful note-taking; careful listening; and a primary concern with HOCs, though with a concurrent sense of when to pay attention to and when to defer LOCs. Whether tutoring in typical writing center one-to-one settings, or tutoring in a writing fellows program, or even facilitating peer response in the classroom, Sam's methods have much to offer.

The uneasy relationship between all participants from Team One provides complex, somewhat troubling, and yet equally important implications for this study. Julian's sense of himself—even during his limited classroom presence during peer reviews—as "reserved advisor" and the gross lack of communication between he and Anne combined to co-construct this cautionary tale of CBT. Julian did not attend class, or even stay in regular communication, enough to know the nuances of Anne's expectations very well. Yet in all his interactions with students, he still tried hard to stay within what he felt were her expectations (primarily via assignment prompts and what students were *telling* him they thought Anne wanted). Anne felt that the lack of communication was all her fault and repeatedly during our interview expressed regret for not interacting more closely with Julian. But she also intimated that she felt students and Julian did not get to know each other well enough on an individual basis to enable Julian to move past his nondirective approach toward a method that might take into account the more individualistic needs of each student. Still, I find great value in this cautionary tale, value that points to our growth and development as a (sub)field. Like Lauren Fitzgerald and Melissa Ianetta, I "take it as a sign of writing center studies' increasing sense of its own identity, as well as its increasing security as a field of study, that we can admit such 'failures' and then move on to create productive, important knowledge from these events" (9). In their laudable work on writing center assessment, Ellen Schendel and William Macauley agree "It is necessary that we become able to accept mistakes and doubts for ourselves ..." and add, "yet it is not sufficient. We have a responsibility to others, as well, especially those for whom we are connections to the field, representatives of how our field works, leaders in our local centers, regional writing center communities, and beyond" (173-74). Julian's experiences also have something to contribute to discussions of writing teachers'/tutors' education and development. His intelligence coupled with his desire to help cannot be denied. But some of Julian's personality traits may make him (and tutors with similar traits) more suitable as an in-class tutor. (And I would say the same, to some degree, about Madeleine.) Julian is expressive and loves to engage in stimulating conversation. It was apparent in his one-to-one tutorials that if the students had been as verbose as he, than the dynamics of the tutorials might have been very different. Especially with this group of students, Julian might have served a better instructional niche if he had been an in-class tutor. There his ability to talk with some fluency about the texts, to offer his opinions and counter-opinions could have been put to better use.

Taken, in sum, Teams Five and Six from Chapter Four—in stark contrast to Team One—offer the true promise of CBT. The participants from Team Five and Six represent what I would classify as organic, home-grown partnerships that took full advantage of the teaching and learning situations they were engaged in. As one of the leaders of the writing program at SCSU, I was put into a position of authority and decision-making outside of the writing center. So instead of recruiting tutors from writing centers, as I did at the UW, I recruited students directly from the same sort of developmental course they would subsequently tutor in. These tutors took the collaborative lessons they learned from having recently taken the course themselves and paid them forward to fellow students they mirrored the diversity of—allowing, importantly—for a closer zone of proximal development and a more truly peer-to-peer learning ecology. The participants in Team Five and Six illustrate what can occur when trust and care are taken to the next level.

Returning to those *Framework* habits of mind mentioned in the Introduction, the results from Team Six seem highly promising: Curiosity? Check. Openness? Check. Engagement? Check. Creativity? Check. And so forth ... Two tutors and an instructor who could care less about whether they were being (or allowing others to be) too directive or nondirective, too controlling or intrusive in their pedagogical interventions ended up realizing a fruitful balance. As with Gina from Team Five and Madeleine from Team Three, their only real concern seemed to be: what can I do to help these students grow and develop confidence and perhaps some competence in their writing performances for that particular course? In the process, we saw Team Six (and to some extent Teams Three and Five) also approaching and pushing the boundaries of their expertise—pushing, especially, the conceived notions of what their roles and authority can or should be. We saw what can happen when young developing writers, thinkers and learners trust in their own authority and take some initiative. The "American Dream Museum Exhibit" assignment vividly showcases the potential of tutors leading the charge, blurring the lines between tutor, student, and teacher—pushing conventional pedagogical boundaries. In collaboratively conceiving of and designing the assignment, Kim and Penny thoughtfully and thought-provokingly scaffolded interactive, problem-posing activities that challenged all students, while at the same time providing ample instructional support—even when the structurally-sanctioned authority of the course, Jake, was not physically present.

In the spirit of "where are they now?" I'd like to briefly report on what I know about the tutors. From the UW tutors, Sam applied and was accepted into a Ph.D. program in English with a focus on Composition and Rhetoric at a major, Midwest research university. For the SCSU tutors, as of April 2013, Gina is a graduate student at the University of Connecticut School of Social Work, working on her master's degree. When I asked her if she thought her experience with CBT has had any lasting effects she wrote:

> Today I have a major role in establishing better policies and procedures for an organization that works with abused children. With the confidence I gained from course-based

> tutoring I have done extremely well at my internship. I have supervisors and program managers asking for my feedback and opinion in changing and establishing new policies. During course-based tutoring I gained a voice that I continue to use today. I am currently at a point in my life where I would have never imagined myself being. I have always been a driven person but never a confident person until I participated in course-based tutoring.

Penny is finishing her Elementary Education requirements as a student teacher. She felt that her experiences with course-based tutoring helped prepare her for her recent successes and future goals: she was captain of the SCSU field hockey team; she studied abroad in Brisbane, Australia, and traveled through the country; and she hoped to return to SCSU in Fall 2013 to get her master's and have her own classroom by Fall of 2014. Like Bradley Hughes, Paula Gillespie, and Harvey Kail, in "What They Take with Them," I believe that the lessons learned, lessons in responsible leadership and mentorship, clear communication, and reflective practice will travel far beyond those courses, for all participants.

CHOICE MATTERS: RECOMMENDATIONS FOR CBT DESIGN AND IMPLEMENTATION

This book's central research question asked: How can what we know about peer tutoring one-to-one and in small groups—especially the implications of directive and nondirective tutoring strategies and methods brought to light in these case studies—inform our work with students in writing centers and other tutoring programs, as well as in classrooms? In answer, this book explored a myriad of ways that tutors in a variety of situations negotiated directive and nondirective strategies while trying to build rapport and trust with fellow students and instructors. In sum, and with the caveat that context might influence the feasibility of any given choice, I offer the following suggestions involving some of the strategic choices CBT practitioners have for successful practice with one-to-one and small-group tutorials, as well other possible classroom activities. These choices radiate from my suggestions for overall design and planning (Figure 5). Some suggestions might also be applicable to other related pedagogical practices, for example: teacher-student conferences, both one-to-one and small-group; writing center tutoring, again both one-to-one and in small groups; or writing classroom collaborative and group activities. (Note that some suggestions for one-to-one tutoring also apply to small-group peer response and vice-versa.)

Overall Design and Planning

- Instructors and tutors should be made aware of *different models of CBT*, both more (tutors like Megan, Madeleine, Gina, Kim, and Penny attending class every day) and less (tutors like Sam not attending class and/or not doing the readings) collaborative designs. Then they should be allowed to choose, as closely as possible, which model they feel might best work for them.
- Have an *early meeting between instructor and tutor* (and coordinator perhaps) during which some tentative roles and expectations are laid out in advance. Be sure to let students know what these roles and expectations are as early as possible.
- Participants should *talk, plan, and reflect with each other on a regular basis*, via email, phone, or face-to-face. Frequent meetings, or online chat forums (blackboard, Skype, or even Facebook, for example) could be used to help facilitate dialogue and communication.
- Directors and coordinators should consider *ongoing development and education* just as important as initial orientations. Tutors could be asked to read current (as in the work of Thompson and colleagues) and/or foundational (like Harris's "Talking") articles in writing center and composition journals during any down time.
- As with the *Framework* and accompanying WPA Outcomes Statement, CBT practitioners, in relation to their respective programs, could develop *learning outcomes or goals*. I would suggest starting with Harris's four aspects for how tutors can assist writers, mentioned repeatedly throughout this book, that she gleaned from hundreds of student responses and years of ground-breaking research and practice. These goals could incorporate the *Framework* habits of mind more generally, and other teaching/learning needs of tutors, tutees, and centers/institutions more specifically. Participant attitudes and other "incipient actions" (Burke *Philosophy* 1, 10-11, 168-9, 379-82; *Grammar* 235-47, 294; *Rhetoric* 50, 90-5) could thereby be coordinated with desired teaching and learning outcomes. These goals can then help guide tutor education courses, and continuing director/tutor development.

One-to-One Tutoring

- Whether tutors attend class every day or sometimes or not at all—if tutors will be conducting one-to-one tutorials outside of class—*have*

students sign up for one-to-ones early in the term so that students and tutor get to know each other as early as possible and so that dialogue about students and the curriculum can start ASAP.
- Students can be offered *shorter 25-minute, or longer 50-minute appointments*, or their choice of either given the situation.
- Tutors should read a student writer's entire paper before making definitive comments. While reading (whether or not the tutor or tutee reads aloud), tutors can take *detailed notes*—a descriptive outline could be especially helpful—and ask students to either take notes as well or follow along and help construct notes with the tutor (and perhaps audio-record the session on their smartphone). We saw all of these moves showcased in detail by Sam during her tutorials in Chapter Three.
- Tutors should be familiar with the intricacies of the *directive/nondirective continuum* in relation to one-to-one tutoring—and develop strategies for negotiating when to be more directive and when to be more facilitative.

Peer Response Facilitation

- If tutors and students are unfamiliar with each other, tutors might allow for some light-hearted banter or *casual conversation* so participants might warm up to one another before getting to the task at hand as we saw happening especially with Teams Five and Six in Chapter Four.
- Tutors should practice *a mix of directive suggestions and modeling with nondirective open-ended questions and follow-up questions* (as we vividly saw with Megan in Chapter Four) so that student writers receive the benefits of specific modeling and so they can also take ownership of their own and their peer group members' learning.
- Tutors should allow for plenty of *wait-time and pauses* during peer response sessions, in order to allow enough time for students to process information and formulate a response (similar to how Sam allowed for during one-to-one tutorials).
- Instructors can experiment with *various elements of peer response* including: having students balance between how much writing versus how much conversation they engage in, and how much and in what ways instructors and tutors intervene and interact with each group in and out of the classroom (see Corbett, LaFrance, and Decker; Corbett and LaFrance *Student*; Corbett "Great").

Figure 5: CBT choices.

Other Classroom Activities

- Tutors do not necessarily need to be in class on a day-to-day basis. What's more important is that when they are there, *all participants have a role to play* and everyone knows what they are.
- *Tutor personalities can be utilized* on their own terms, but instructors can also foster interpersonal opportunities that might expand tutor approaches to interacting with fellow students. Shyer tutors (or students holding back, like Megan), for example, could be gently encouraged to speak up in class if they feel they have something important to contribute. More talkative students (like Madeleine) could be nudged to balance their comments with questions and prompts that might encourage other students in class to participate or take

intellectual risks.

- Tutors can be encouraged to *take some authority and ownership* in the design and orchestration of the class: they can help design and lead the implementation of lesson plans and assignments as we saw with Team Six; and they can share their own writing and learning experiences, strategies and processes liberally with their peers as we saw especially with Teams Five and Six.

LOOKING BACK WHILE LOOKING FORWARD: DIVERSITY AND CHOICE IN RECRUITMENT, RESEARCH QUESTIONS, AND ASSESSMENT

This study has also made me question how, where, and why we recruit peer tutors. I believe—like Nelson—that we should seriously consider concerted efforts toward recruiting for more diversity in centers and programs that have been staffed predominantly by mainstream students. Though the data clearly show that a white, mainstream tutor can identify and assist nonmainstream and diverse students, as in the case of Megan and especially Sam and Penny, we clearly saw the benefits of having a tutor like Madeleine, a tutor who did indeed mirror the UW EOP students' diversity, or a tutor like Gina, who struggles with an LD like the student Max, working closely with their peers. Students like Madeleine, Gina, Kim, and Penny—students who themselves took the developmental course, who learned lessons in how to navigate that course successfully—offer an exceptionally promising model of mirroring peer diversity that takes Vygotsky's ZPD closely to heart. The cover image of this book—the Roman god Janus on a priceless coin—symbolizes the value of that promise. Double-faced Janus, looking simultaneously forward and backward in time, was the god of transitions, journeys, doors, gates, boundaries, endings, and beginnings. This book has offered intimate gazes into the developmental transitions of students, tutors, instructors, and researcher. Readers might look back on what this book has to offer as they look forward in their programmatic and pedagogical decision making: boundary-pushing between writing centers/peer tutoring programs and classrooms, between directive/nondirective instruction, between what it means to be a teacher/student. A student like Gina who works closely under an instructor like Mya with students/future tutors like Kim and Penny provides an example of interpersonal continuity from course to course and student/tutor to student/tutor. Further, this model can provide insights into how diverse students transition from high school to college writing and learning environments, especially if we listen closely to their stories. Yet we might consider a more advanced student like Sam as a diverse tutor herself due to the fact that she was a double major. When Sam originally applied and interviewed to be a peer tutor for the English Department Writing Center, she was not hired by the director. Later, while recruiting course-based tutors, I re-interviewed Sam. Despite feeling that her personality was a bit too "low key," I brought her aboard anyway. Perhaps her multifarious experiences in navigating writing course boundaries and intersections between the humanities and natural sciences aided in her salutary tutoring strategies (see Thaiss and Zawacki 106). Maybe her low-key demeanor contributed to her commendable listening skills. If diverse students in their many guises do not apply to be tutors, then we should search them out—actively recruiting for talent and cultural and academic diversity—for our diverse writing programs, centers, and classrooms.

Once we've recruited for as much diversity and talent as possible, we can then make relevant choices on where and how to focus our research and assessment. I have advocated for a multi-method approach whenever possible, one that, if you will, methodologically mirrors the diversity of the participants involved in CBT-inspired research and practices. I want to see some researchers continue to focus on the sorts of pragmatic questions of tutoring style and method that have generated RAD case-study research from Spigelman, Thompson and colleagues, White-Farnham, Dyehouse and Finer, me, and others. I also want us to continue to build usable, authentic means of assessment that can help CBT practitioners successfully close the assessment loop, uniting learning outcomes with the habits of mind that undergird and can open the doors to successful, satisfying teaching and writing performances (see Schendel and Macauley; Johnson). But I hope others will continue to stay open and curious when they begin to hear boundary-pushing stories that warrant following up on. And when the chance arises to do both, I want our field(s) to embrace the multi-perspectives that multi-method research can deliver. By staying open, curious, and persistent in our efforts toward more hybrid, multi-method research, we can provide for more of the types of authentic assessment that can link creative processes and performances, habits of mind, identity formations, and student, teacher, and instructor success and satisfaction.

We have choices in our quests for synergistic teaching, learning, and trust. And we should welcome all colleagues, at all levels—slow and fast—ready and willing to accompany us in our journeys.

WORKS CITED

Anderson, Julie Aipperspach, and Susan Wolff Murphy. "Bringing the Writing Center into the Classroom: A Case Study of Writing Groups." Moss, Highberg, and Nicolas 47-62. Print.

Babcock, Rebecca Day, and Terese Thonus. *Researching the Writing Center: Towards an Evidence-Based Practice.* New York: Peter Lang, 2012. Print.

Barber-Fendley, Kimber, and Chris Hamel. "A New Visibility: An Argument for Alternative Assistance Programs for Students with Learning Disabilities." *College Composition and Communication* 55.3 (2004): 504-35. Print.

Barnett, Robert W., and Jacob S. Blumner, eds. *The Allyn and Bacon Guide to Writing Center Theory and Practice.* Needham Heights, MA: Allyn and Bacon, 2001. Print.

Beaufort, Anne. *College Writing and Beyond: A New Framework for University Writing Instruction.* Logan, UT: Utah State UP, 2007. Print.

Bishop, Wendy. "Helping Peer Writing Groups Succeed." *Teaching English in the Two-Year College* 15 (1988): 120-25. Print.

Black, Laurel Johnson. *Between Talk and Teaching: Reconsidering the Writing Conference.* Logan: Utah State UP, 1998. Print.

Blum-Kulka, Shoshana. "Discourse Pragmatics." *Discourse as Social Interaction.* Ed. Teun A. Van Dijk. London: Sage, 1997. 38-63. Print.

Boquet, Elizabeth H. "Intellectual Tug-of-War: Snapshots of Life in the Center." *Stories from the Center: Connecting Narrative and Theory in the Writing Center.* Ed. Briggs Lynne Craigue, and Meg Woolbright. Urbana, IL: NCTE, 2000. 17-30. Print.

---. *Noise from the Writing Center.* Logan: Utah State UP, 2002. Print.

Boquet, Elizabeth H. and Neal Lerner. "Reconsiderations: After 'The Idea of a Writing Center.'" *College English* 71.2 (Nov. 2008): 170-89. Print.

Brooke, Robert, Ruth Mirtz, and Rick Evans. *Small Groups in Writing Workshops: Invitations to a Writer's Life.* Urbana, IL: NCTE, 1994. Print.

Brooks, Jeff. "Minimalist Tutoring: Making the Students Do All the Work." *The Writing Lab Newsletter* 15.6 (1991): 1-4. Print.

Bruffee, Kenneth A. *Collaborative Learning: Higher Education, Interdependence, and the Authority of Knowledge.* 2nd ed. Baltimore: The John Hopkins UP, 1999. Print.

---. A *Short Course in Writing: Composition, Collaborative Learning, and Constructive Reading* 4th ed. New York: Pearson, 2007. Print.

Bruland, Holly Huff. "'Accomplishing Intellectual Work': An Investigation of the Re-Locations Enacted through On-Location Tutoring." *Praxis: A Writing Center Journal* 4.2 (Spring 2007). Web. 1 Jan. 2015.

Buranen, Lise, and Alice M. Roy, eds. *Perspectives on Plagiarism and Intellectual Property in a Postmodern World.* SUNY UP, 1999. Print.

Burke, Kenneth. *A Grammar of Motives.* New York: Prentice Hall, 1945. Print.

---. *The Philosophy of Literary Form: Studies in Symbolic Action.* Berkeley: U of California P, 1973 (Orig. pub. 1941). Print.

---. *A Rhetoric of Motives.* Berkeley: U of California P, 1969 (Orig. pub. 1950). Print.

Cairns, Rhoda, and Paul V. Anderson. "The Protean Shape of the Writing Associate's Role: An Empirical Study and Conceptual Model." *Across the Disciplines* 5 (March 29, 2008). Web. 1 Jan. 2015.

Carillo, Ellen "Teaching Academic Integrity and Critical Thinking through Collaboration." Corbett, LaFrance, and Decker 65-76. Print.

Carino, Peter. "Power and Authority in Peer Tutoring." *The Center Will Hold: Critical Perspectives on Writing Center Scholarship.* Ed. Michael A. Pemberton, and Joyce Kinkead. Logan: Utah State UP, 2003. 96-116. Print.

Carroll, Lee Ann. *Rehearsing New Roles: How College Students Develop as Writers.* Carbondale: Southern Illinois University Press, 2002. Print.

Cazden, Courtney B. *Classroom Discourse: The Language of Teaching and Learning* 2nd ed. Portsmouth, NH: Heinemann, 2001. Print.

Chig, Cory Lawson. "The Instructor-Led Peer Conference: Teachers as Participants in Peer Response." Corbett, LaFrance, and Decker 15-28. Print.

Clark, Irene Lurkis. "Collaboration and Ethics in Writing Center Pedagogy." *The Writing Center Journal* 9.1 (1988): 3-12. Print.

---. "Perspectives on the Directive/Non-Directive Continuum in the Writing Center." *The Writing Center Journal* 22.1 (2001): 33-58. Print.

---. "Writing Centers and Plagiarism." Buranen and Roy 155-167. Print.

Clark, Irene Lurkis, and Dave Healy. "Are Writing Centers Ethical?" Barnett and Blumner 242-59. Orig. published in *WPA: Writing Program Administration* 20 (1996): 32-38. Print.

Cogie, Jane, Dawn Janke, Teresa Joy Kramer, and Chad Simpson. "Risks in Collaboration: Accountability as We Move beyond the Center's Walls." *Marginal Words, Marginal Work? Tutoring the Academy in the Work of Writing Centers.* Ed. William J Macauley Jr., and Nicholas Mauriello. Cresskill, NJ: Hampton, 2007. 105-34. Print.

Cooper, Marilyn M. "Really Useful Knowledge: A Cultural Studies Agenda for Writing Centers." *The Writing Center Journal* 14.2 (1994): 97-111. Print.

Corbett, Steven J. "Bringing the Noise: Peer Power and Authority, On Location." Spigelman and Grobman 101-111. Print.

---. "Great Debating: Combining Ancient and Contemporary Methods of Peer Critique." PraxisWiki. *Kairos: A Journal of Rhetoric, Technology, and Pedagogy* (October 8, 2014). Web. 1 Jan. 2015.

---. "Learning Disability and Response-Ability: Reciprocal Caring in Developmental Peer Response Writing Groups and Beyond." *Pedagogy: Critical Approaches to Teaching Literature, Language, Composition, and Culture.* 15.3 (Spring 2015): 61-85.

---."Negotiating Pedagogical Authority: The Rhetoric of Writing Center Tutoring Styles and Methods." *Rhetoric Review* 32.1 (2013): 81-98. Print.

---. "The Role of the Emissary: Helping to Bridge the Communication Canyon between Instructors and Students." *The Writing Lab Newsletter* 27.2 (Oct. 2002): 10-11. Print.

---."Tutoring Style, Tutoring Ethics: The Continuing Relevance of the Directive/Nondirective Instructional Debate." *Praxis: A Writing Center Journal* 5.2 (Spring 2008)Web. 1 Jan. 2015. Rpt. in the *St. Martin's Sourcebook for Writing Tutors* 4th ed. Ed. Christina Murphy, and Steve Sherwood. Boston: Bedford/St Martin's, 2011. 148-155. Print.

---."Using Case Study Multi-Methods to Investigate Close(r) Collaboration: Course-Based Tutoring and the Directive/Nondirective Instructional Continuum." *The Writing Center Journal* 31.1 (2011): 55-81. Print.

---. "Writing Center Research in the Making: Questioning Hierarchies of Authority across the Curriculum." Paper Presented at the 2nd International Conference on Writing Research. Santa Barbara, CA. February, 2005.

Corbett, Steven J., and Juan C. Guerra. "Collaboration and Play in the Writing Classroom." *Academic Exchange Quarterly* 9.4 (Winter 2005): 106-11. Print.

Corbett, Steven J., and Michelle LaFrance. "From Grammatical to Global: The WAC/Writing Center Connection." *Praxis: A Writing Center Journal* 6.2 (Spring 2009). Web. 1 Jan. 2015.

---, eds. *Student Peer Review and Response: A Critical Sourcebook.* New York/ Boston: Bedford/St. Martin's, Forthcoming.

Corbett, Steven J., Michelle LaFrance, and Teagan Decker, eds. *Peer Pressure, Peer Power: Theory and Practice in Peer Review and Response for the Writing Classroom.* Southlake, TX: Fountainhead Press, 2014. Print.

Corbett, Steven J., Sydney F. Lewis, and Madeleine M. Clifford. "Diversity Matters in Individualized Instruction: The Pros and Cons of Team Teaching and Talkin' that Talk." *Diversity in the Composition Classroom.* Ed. Gwendolyn Hale, Mike Mutschelknaus, and Thomas Alan Holmes. Southlake, TX: Fountainhead Press, 2010. 85-96. Print.

Corroy, Jennifer. "Institutional Change and the University of Wisconsin—Madison Writing Fellows Program." Spigelman and Grobman 205-18. Print.

Daiker, Donald A. "Learning to Praise." *Writing and Response: Theory, Practice, and Research*. Ed. Chris M. Anson. Urbana, IL: NCTE, 1989. 103-13. Print.

Decker, Teagan. "Academic (Un)Seriousness: How Tutor Talk Plays with Academic Discourse" *The Writing Lab Newsletter* 30.4 (Dec. 2005): 11-13. Print.

---."Diplomatic Relations: Peer Tutors in the Writing Classroom." Spigelman and Grobman 17-30. Print.

Delpit, Lisa. *Other People's Children: Cultural Conflict in the Classroom* 2nd ed. New York: The New Press, 2006. Print.

---."The Silenced Dialogue: Power and Pedagogy in Educating Other People's Children." *Harvard Educational Review* 58.3 (Aug. 1988): 280-97. Print.

Denny, Harry C. *Facing the Center: Toward an Identity Politics of One-to-One Mentoring*. Logan: Utah State UP, 2010. Print.

DiPardo, Anne. "'Whispers of Coming and Going': Lessons from Fannie." *The Writing Center Journal* 12.2 (1992): 125-44. Print.

Driscoll, Dana, and Sherry Wynn Perdue. "Theory, Lore, and More: An Analysis of RAD Research in *The Writing Center Journal*, 1980-2009." *The Writing Center Journal* 32.1 (2012): 11-39.

Dylan, Bob. "The Times They Are A-Changin.'" *The Times They Are A-Changin.'* Columbia, 1964. CD.

Ender, Steven C., and Fred B. Newton. *Students Helping Students: A Guide for Peer Educators on College Campuses.* San Francisco, CA: Jossey-Bass, 2000. Print.

Fitzgerald, Lauren. "Writing Center Scholarship: A 'Big Cross-Disciplinary Tent.'" *Exploring Composition Studies: Sites, Issues, and Perspectives.* Ed. Kelly Ritter, and Paul Kei Matsuda. Logan, UT: Utah State UP, 2012. 73-88. Print.

Fitzgerald, Lauren, and Melissa Ianetta. "From the Editors." *The Writing Center Journal* 32.2 (2012): 9-10. Print.

Framework for Success in Postsecondary Writing. Developed jointly by the Council of Writing Program Administrators, the National Council of Teachers of English, and the National Writing Project, 2011. Web. 1 Jan. 2015.

Freire, Paulo. *Pedagogy of Freedom: Ethics, Democracy, and Civic Courage*. Oxford: Rowman and Littlefield, 1998. Print.

Geller, Anne Ellen, Michele Eodice, Frankie Condon, Meg Carroll, and Elizabeth H. Boquet. *The Everyday Writing Center: A Community of Practice*. Logan: Utah State UP, 2007. Print.

Gerben, Chris. "Make it Work: *Project Runway* as Model and Metaphor of Authority and Expertise." Corbett, LaFrance, and Decker 29-42. Print.

Gere, Anne Ruggles, and Ralph Stevens. "The Language of Writing Groups: How Oral Response Shapes Revision." *The Acquisition of Written Language: Response and Revision*. Ed. Sarah Warshauer Freedman. Norwood, NJ: Ablex,

1985. 85-105.
Gilewicz, Magdalena. "Sponsoring Student Response in Writing Center Group Tutorials." Moss, Highberg, and Nicolas 63-78. Print.
Gilewicz, Magdalena, and Terese Thonus. "Close Vertical Transcription in Writing Center Training and Research." *The Writing Center Journal* 24.1 (2003): 25-49. Print.
Gillespie, Paula, and Neal Lerner. *The Allyn and Bacon Guide to Peer Tutoring* 2nd ed. New York: Pearson, 2004. Print.
Goffman, Erving. *Forms of Talk*. Philadelphia: U of Pennsylvania P, 1981. Print.
Greenfield, Laura and Karen Rowan, eds. *Writing Centers and the New Racism: A Call for Sustainable Dialogue and Change*. Logan: Utah State UP, 2011. Print.
Grimm, Nancy Maloney. *Good Intentions: Writing Center Work for Postmodern Times*. Portsmouth, NH: Boynton/Cook, 1999. Print.
Grutsch McKinney, Jackie. *Peripheral Visions for Writing Centers*. Logan: Utah State UP, 2013. Print.
Hafer, Gary R. "Ideas in Practice: Supplemental Instruction in Freshman Composition." *The Journal of Developmental Education* 24 (2001): 30-37. Print.
Hall, Emily, and Bradley Hughes. "Preparing Faculty, Professionalizing Fellows: Keys to Success with Undergraduate Writing Fellows in WAC." *The WAC Journal* 22 (2011): 21-40. Print.
Haring-Smith, Tori. "Changing Students' Attitudes: Writing Fellows Programs." *Writing Across the Curriculum: A Guide to Developing Programs*. Ed. Susan McLeod, and Margot Soven. Newbury Park, CA: Sage, 1992. 175-88. Print.
Harris, Muriel. "Centering in on Professional Choices." *College Composition and Communication* 52.3 (Feb. 2001): 429-40. Print.
---. "Collaboration Is Not Collaboration Is Not Collaboration: Writing Center vs. Peer-Response Groups." *College Composition and Communication* 43 (1992): 369-83. Print.
---. "A Non-Coda: Including Writing Centered Student Perspectives for Peer Review." Corbett, LaFrance, and Decker 277-88. Print.
---. "Talking in the Middle: Why Writers Need Writing Tutors." *College English* 57.1 (Jan. 1995): 27-42. Print.
---. *Teaching One-to-One: The Writing Conference*. Urbana, IL: NCTE, 1986. Print.
Haswell, Richard H. "NCTE/CCCC's Recent War of Scholarship." *Written Communication* 22.2 (2005): 198-223. Print.
Healy, Dave. "A Defense of Dualism: The Writing Center and the Classroom." *The Writing Center Journal* 14.1 (1993): 16-29. Print.
Hemmeter, Thomas. "The 'Smack of Difference': The Language of Writing Center Discourse." *The Writing Center Journal* 11.1 (1990): 35-48. Print.

Hughes, Bradley, Paula Gillespie, and Harvey Kail. "What They Take with Them: Findings from the Peer Tutor Alumni Research Project." *The Writing Center Journal* 30.2 (2010): 12-46. Print.

Hurley, Maureen, Glen Jacobs, and Melinda Gilbert. "The Basic SI Model." *Supplemental Instruction: New Visions for Empowering Student Learning.* Ed. Marion E. Stone and Glen Jacobs. San Francisco, CA: Jossey-Bass, 2006. 11-22. Print.

Johnson, Kristine. "Beyond Standards: Disciplinary and National Perspectives on Habits of Mind." *College Composition and Communication* 64.3 (Feb. 2013): 517-41. Print.

Kail, Harvey, and John Trimbur. "The Politics of Peer Tutoring." *The Writing Center Journal* 11.1-2 (1987): 5-12. Print.

Kilborn, Judith. "Cultural Diversity in the Writing Center: Defining Ourselves and Our Challenges." Barnett and Blumner 391-400. Orig. published in *The Writing Lab Newsletter* 19.1 (1994): 7-10. Print.

Launspach, Sonja. "The Role of Talk in Small Writing Groups: Building Declarative and Procedural Knowledge for Basic Writers." *Journal of Basic Writing* 27.2 (2008): 56-78. Print.

Lawfer, Laura. "Writing Fellows: An Innovative Approach to Tutoring." *The Writing Lab Newsletter* 29.9 (2005): 12-13, 10. Print.

Lee, Carol D. "Double Voiced Discourse: African American Vernacular English as Resource in Cultural Modeling Classrooms." *Bakhtinian Perspectives on Language, Literacy, and Learning.* Ed. Arentha F. Ball, and Sarah Warshauer Freedman. Cambridge: Cambridge UP. 129-47. Print.

Lerner, Neal. *The Idea of a Writing Laboratory*. Carbondale: Southern Illinois UP, 2009. Print.

---. "The Teacher-Student Writing Conference and the Desire for Intimacy." *College English* 68.2 (Nov. 2005): 186-208. Print.

Liggett, Sarah, Kerri Jordan, and Steve Price. "Mapping Knowledge-Making in Writing Center Research: A Taxonomy of Methodologies." *The Writing Center Journal* 31.2 (2011): 50-88. Print.

Liu, Barbara Little, and Holly Mandes. "The Idea of a Writing Center Meets the Reality of Classroom-Based Tutoring." Spigelman and Grobman 87-100. Print.

Lutes, Jean Marie. "Why Feminists Make Better Tutors: Gender and Disciplinary Expertise in a Curriculum-Based Tutoring Program." *Writing Center Research: Extending the Conversation.* Ed. Paula Gillespie, Alice Gillam, Lady Falls Brown, and Byron Stay. Mahwah, NJ: Lawrence Erlbaum Associates, 2002. 235-57. Print.

Mackiewicz, Jo, and Isabelle Kramer Thompson. *Talk about Writing: The Tu-*

toring Strategies of Experienced Writing Center Tutors. New York: Routledge, 2015. Print.

Mann, April. "Structure and Accommodation: Autism and the Writing Center." *Autism Spectrum Disorders in the College Composition Classroom: Making Writing Instruction More Accessible for All Students.* Ed. Val Gerstle, and Lynda Walsh. Milwaukee, WI: Marquette UP, 2011. 43-74. Print.

Miller, Judith E., James E. Groccia, and Marilyn S. Miller, eds. *Student-Assisted Teaching: A Guide to Faculty-Student Teamwork.* Bolton, MA: Anker, 2001. Print.

Moss, Beverly J., Nels P. Highberg, and Melissa Nicolas, eds. *Writing Groups Inside and Outside the Classroom.* Mahwah, NJ: Lawrence Erlbaum Associates, 2004. Print.

Murphy, Susan Wolff. "'Just Check It: I Mean, Don't Get Fixed on It': Self Presentation in Writing Center Discourse." *The Writing Center Journal* 26.1 (2006): 62-82. Print.

Neff, Julie. "Learning Disabilities and the Writing Center." *Intersections: Theory-Practice in the Writing Center.* Ed. Joan A. Mullin and Ray Wallace. Urbana, IL: NCTE, 1994. 81-95. Print.

Nelson, Marie Wilson. *At the Point of Need: Teaching Basic and ESL Writers.* Portsmouth, NH: Boynton/Cook, 1991. Print.

Nelson, Jane, and Margaret Garner. "Horizontal Structures for Learning." *Before and After the Tutorial: Writing Centers and Institutional Relationships.* Ed. Nicholas Mauriello, William J. Macauley, Jr., and Robert T. Koch, Jr. New York: Hampton, 2011. 7-27. Print.

Nicolas, Melissa. "A Cautionary Tale about 'Tutoring' Peer Response Groups." Spigelman and Grobman 112-25. Print.

North, Stephen M. "The Idea of a Writing Center." *College English* 46.5 (1984): 433-46. Print.

---. "Revisiting 'The Idea of a Writing Center.'" *Writing Center Journal* 15.1 (1994): 7-19. Print.

Paulson, Eric J., Jonathan Alexander, and Sonya Armstrong. "Peer Review Re-Reviewed: Investigating the Juxtaposition of Composition Students' Eye Movements and Peer-Review Processes." *Research in the Teaching of English* 41.3 (Feb. 2007): 304-35. Print.

Pemberton, Michael A. "Introduction to 'The Function of Talk in the Writing Conference: A Study of Tutorial Conversation.'" *The Writing Center Journal* 30.1 (2010): 23-26. Print.

Raines, Helon Howell. "Tutoring and Teaching: Continuum, Dichotomy, or Dialectic?" *The Writing Center Journal* 14.2 (1994): 150-62. Print.

Reid, E. Shelley. "Peer Review for Peer Review's Sake: Resituating Peer Review

Pedagogy." Corbett, LaFrance, and Decker 217-31. Print.

Robinson, Heather M., and Jonathan Hall. "Connecting WID and the Writing Center: Tools for Collaboration." *The WAC Journal* 24 (2013): 29-47.

Schendel, Ellen, and William J. Macauley, Jr. *Building Writing Center Assessments that Matter*. Logan: Utah State UP, 2012. Print.

Schunk, Dale H. *Learning Theories: An Educational Perspective* 4th ed. Columbus, OH: Pearson/Merrill Prentice Hall, 2004. Print.

Severino, Carol. "Rhetorically Analyzing Collaborations." *The Writing Center Journal* 13 (1992): 53-64. Print.

Severino, Carol, and Mary Trachsel. "Theories of Specialized Discourses and Writing Fellows Programs." *Across the Disciplines* 5 (March 29, 2008).Web. 1 Jan. 2015.

Shamoon, Linda K., and Deborah H. Burns. "A Critique of Pure Tutoring." *The Writing Center Journal* 15.2 (1995): 134-52. Print.

Shaparenko, Bithyah. "Focus on Focus: How to Facilitate Discussion in a Peer Group." *The Writing Lab Newsletter* 29.8 (2005): 11-12. Print.

Smith, Louise Z. "Independence and Collaboration: Why We Should Decentralize Writing Centers." *The Writing Center Journal* 23.2 (2003): 15-23. Orig. pub. in 7.1 (1986): 3-10. Print.

Smitherman, Geneva. *Talkin and Testifyin: The Language of Black America*. Detroit, MI: Wayne State UP, 1977. Print.

Smulyan, Lisa, and Kristen Bolton. "Classroom and Writing Center Collaborations: Peers as Authorities." *The Writing Center Journal* 9.2 (1989): 43-49. Print.

Soliday, Mary. *Everyday Genres: Writing Assignments across the Disciplines*. Carbondale and Edwardsville: Southern Illinois UP, 2011. Print.

---. "Shifting Roles in Classroom Tutoring: Cultivating the Art of Boundary Crossing." *The Writing Center Journal* 16.1 (1995): 59-73. Print.

Soven, Margot Iris. "Curriculum-Based Peer Tutoring Programs: A Survey." *Writing Program Administration* 17.1-2 (1993): 58-74. Print.

Spigelman, Candace. "Reconstructing Authority: Negotiating Power in Democratic Learning Sites." Spigelman and Grobman 185-204. Print.

---. "'Species' of Rhetoric: Deliberative and Epideictic Models in Writing Center Settings." Moss, Highberg, and Nicolas 133-50. Print.

---. "The Ethics of Appropriation in Peer Writing Groups." Buranen and Roy 231-40. Print.

Spigelman, Candace and Laurie Grobman, eds. *On Location: Theory and Practice in Classroom-Based Writing Tutoring*. Logan: Utah State UP, 2005. Print.

Spigelman, Candace, and Laurie Grobman. "Introduction: On Location in Classroom-Based Writing Tutoring." Spigelman and Grobman 1-13. Print.

Spilman, Isabel B. "Tutoring Five on Five." *The Writing Lab Newsletter* 13.10 (1989): 9-10. Print.

Stewart, Donald C. "Collaborative Learning: Boon or Bane? *Rhetoric Review* 7 (1988): 58-83. Print.

Thaiss, Chris, and Terry Myers Zawacki. *Engaged Writers and Dynamic Disciplines: Research on the Academic Writing Life.* Portsmouth, NH: Boynton/Cook, 2006. Print.

Thompson, Isabelle. "Scaffolding in the Writing Center: A Microanalysis of an Experienced Tutor's Verbal and Nonverbal Tutoring Strategies." *Written Communication* 26 (2009): 417-53. Print.

Thompson, Isabelle, Alyson Whyte, David Shannon, Amanda Muse, Kristen Miller, MillaChappell, and Abby Whigham. "Examining Our Lore: A Survey of Students' and Tutors' Satisfaction with Writing Center Conferences." *The Writing Center Journal* 29.1 (2009): 78-105. Print.

Thompson, Isabelle, and Jo Mackiewicz. "Questioning in Writing Center Conferences." *The Writing Center Journal* 33.2 (2014): 37-70. Print.

Trimbur, John. "Peer Tutoring: A Contradiction in Terms?" *The Writing Center Journal* 7.2 (1987): 21-28. Print.

Trimbur, John, and Harvey Kail. "Foreword." Bruffee, *A Short Course* xix-xxix. Print.

Vidali, Amy. "Discourses of Disability and Basic Writing." *Disability and the Teaching of Writing: A Critical Sourcebook.* Ed. Cynthia Lewiecki-Wilson, and Brenda Jo Brueggemann. Boston: Bedford/St. Martin's, 2008. 40-55. Print.

Walker, Carolyn, and David Elias. "Writing Conference Talk: Factors Associated with High- and Low-Rated Writing Conferences." *Research in the Teaching of English* 21.3 (1987): 226-85. Print.

White-Farnham, Jamie, Jeremiah Dyehouse, and Bryna Siegel Finer. "Mapping Tutorial Interactions: A Report on Results and Implications." *Praxis: A Writing Center Journal* 9.2 (2012). Web. 1 Jan. 2015.

Zawacki, Terry Myers. "Writing Fellows as WAC Change Agents: Changing What? Changing Whom? Changing How?" *Across the Disciplines* 5 (March 29, 2008).Web. 1 Jan. 2015.

APPENDIX

APPENDIX A: INTERVIEW QUESTIONS FOR INSTRUCTORS AND TUTORS

Instructors

1. Could you tell me just a little about yourself: where you're at in the program, what your area of focus is, how long you've been teaching?
2. So how did it go? What are your overall impressions of your experience with course-based tutoring?
3. What worked well?
4. What were the students' impressions? The tutors?
5. What roles(s) did the course-based tutor play: e.g., instruction partner, conversation participant, discussion leader?
6. Did you require visits to the tutor?
7. How did it compare/contrast to not having a tutor directly attached to the EOP classroom?
8. What might have worked better? What suggestions might you offer other tutors or TAs interested in participating in this project?
9. How did this experience affect your relationship to the Instructional Center or other writing centers?
10. Would you collaborate with a course-based tutor again? Would you make any changes in the way you employed the tutor, to your syllabus or assignments, or in any other way?
11. Did this experience change or add to your overall view of what it means to tutor, teach, or learn writing?

Tutors

1. Could you tell me just a little about yourself: where you're at in your studies, grade level; what your major is; how long you've been tutoring?
2. How did it go? What are your overall impressions of your experience with course-based tutoring?
3. What worked well?
4. What were the students' impressions of your involvement with the class? The TAs?

5. What role(s) did you play: e.g., instruction partner, conversation participant, discussion leader?
6. How did your in-class experience compare/contrast to your experiences as a tutor one-to-one in the Center?
7. What might have worked better? What suggestions might you offer other tutors or TAs interested in participating in this project?
8. Did your tutor training and experience as a one-to-one tutor prepare you for this role?
9. Would you be willing to be a course-based tutor again? What changes, if any would you make, or want to see made?

APPENDIX B: STUDENT QUESTIONNAIRES

This questionnaire asks general questions about your perspectives on interacting with an in-class tutor for this course. Participation is voluntary. You may skip any questions that you do not wish to answer. Your responses will be used to better understand the effects and potential value added by having an in-class tutor. The information you provide here is confidential. Based on your responses, we may contact you in the future to ask if you'd like to participate in a follow-up interview.

1. Before this class, how often would you say you've used peer writing tutors in the past? (check one):

   Often______ Occasionally_____ Rarely______ Never_____

   Comment:

2. What are your overall impressions of having a course-based tutor?
3. What did you like best about having a course-based tutor?
4. Were there any problems with having a course-based tutor?
5. How did this compare to not having a course-based tutor in English 104? [Only for UW case studies]
6. Do you feel that you saw or visited a tutor more or less often than in English 104? [Only for UW case studies]
7. Did you visit your tutor for a one-to-one tutorial? How did this compare to your in-class interactions?
8. Do you think that you will continue to talk to writing tutors in the future?

APPENDIX C: LINGUISTIC FEATURES AND CUES OF ONE-TO-ONE TUTORIALS FOR TEAMS ONE-FOUR

Ling. Feat. and Cues	**Julian** *Team One*	**Students**	**Megan** *Team Two*	**Students**
# of Sessions	6		8/7	
Average Length (minutes)	36		11/18	
Total Words Spoken	15,049	5,835	8,986/ 11,675	2,150/ 2,444
Average # of Words Spoken per Minute	70	27	102/93	24/19
Content-clarifying Questions	20		15/18	
Open-ended Questions	93		12/8	
Directive Questions	8		5/12	
References to TA	14	13	7/17	2/6
References to Assignment Prompt	12	1	1/1	0/0
Interruptions	28	13	8/17	26/20
Main Channel Overlaps	1	4	1/8	5/22
Joint Productions	4	9	3/8	17/23

Ling. Feat. and Cues	**Madeleine** *Team Three*	**Students**	**Sam** *Team Four*	**Students**
# of Sessions	3/1		11	
Average Length (minutes)	50/59		25	
Total Words Spoken	12,115/ 7,614	1,919/ 2,997	18,181	11,292
Average # of Words Spoken per Minute	81/129	13/51	66	41
Content-clarifying Questions	5/4		20	
Open-ended Questions	23/2		137	
Directive Questions	23/5		21	
References to TA	7/4	0/2	1	3
References to Assignment Prompt	1/0	0/1	1	0
Interruptions	21/44	10/50	12	37
Main Channel Overlaps	3/6	7/25	7	12
Joint Productions	3/5	24/6	9	49

APPENDIX D: AMERICAN DREAM MUSEUM EXHIBIT ASSIGNMENT

The American Dream Museum Exhibit

Your team has been asked to create an exhibition that communicates the essence of the American Dream.

Your job is to collect artifacts—images, music, literature, poems, or other items that represent or symbolize the idea behind the American Dream. Use your imagination and have fun!

Each team member must collect ten items and bring them in for discussion with the other team members. You should be able to make an argument about why you believe each artifact should be in the exhibition. Then, the team should **choose five objects from each person's collection.** ***Take notes about why those items were selected as representatives of the American Dream.***

The format of your exhibit is limitless—your team (if everyone can agree) can have an overarching theme such as "Unrealistic Expectations? Women and the American Dream" or "His Way and the American Way: Music and Images of Frank Sinatra" or you can have a hodge-podge collection of items. The important thing to remember is that you must be able to make the argument that your exhibition says something about some aspect of the American Dream.

1. At some point before the exhibit, decide on a title of your exhibition—be creative!
2. Each individual team member will write a one to two page argument about each of their (5) artifacts and why they are important representations of the American Dream. For example, if you are writing about an image, you might do a textual analysis of the image—the subject, composition of the elements, colors, etc. If you selected a song or other music, you might show how the music or lyrics represent the American Dream. Try to make connections and/or cite some of the material we've covered in class.
3. Each team member will also write a one or two page introduction to the exhibit. Be sure to define the "American Dream." (We created a definition in class and our reading materials also defined it.) This introduction should provide an overview of the exhibit and why the audience should be interested in it. Look over all our material from this semester—the founding documents, speeches, and essays. Again, try to connect and/or cite some of the material we've covered in class.

4. Finally, each team will give a tour of their exhibit and provide information about their artifacts.

Due Dates:

Thurs—04/15 Each person brings in ten artifacts—Teams discuss and narrow down each person to 5

Thurs—04/22 Each team member brings in and reads their arguments about each of their artifacts

Thurs—04/29 Teams work on the design and order of their artifacts and presentation

Tues—05/04 Group Project Presentations

Thur—05/06 Group Project Presentations

INDEX

N

R

S

T

V

W

Z

ABOUT THE AUTHOR

Steven J. Corbett is Assistant Professor of English at George Mason University. He received his Ph.D. in English Language and Rhetoric from the University of Washington-Seattle in 2008, and he was assistant professor of English and co-coordinator of composition at Southern Connecticut State University-New Haven from 2008-2013. He is co-editor (with Michelle LaFrance and Teagan Decker) of the collection *Peer Pressure, Peer Power: Theory and Practice in Peer Review and Response for the Writing Classroom* (Fountainhead Press, 2014). His essays on teaching, writing, and rhetoric have appeared in *The Writing Center Journal, Rhetoric Review, Pedagogy, Kairos, The Writing Lab Newsletter, Interdisciplinary Studies in Literature and Environment, The St. Martin's Sourcebook for Writing Tutors* 4th ed., *On Location, Diversity in the Composition Classroom, ePortfolio Performance Support Systems, Inside Higher Ed, The Chronicle of Higher Education*, and elsewhere. He is currently co-editing (with Michelle LaFrance) a forthcoming critical sourcebook on student peer review and response for Bedford/St. Martin's, co-editing (with Betsy Cooper) a special multimodal issue of the journal *Across the Disciplines* on writing in the performing and visual arts, and co-authoring a monograph (with Paul Rogers) on listening and responding to writers and writing.

www.ingramcontent.com/pod-product-compliance
Ingram Content Group UK Ltd.
Pitfield, Milton Keynes, MK11 3LW, UK
UKHW041356190726
13851UKWH00014B/128